BOLD & BEAUTIFUL
Easy-Sew Clothes

Habibe Acikgoz

jacqui small

First published in 2013 by
Jacqui Small LLP
An imprint of Aurum Press
74–77 White Lion Street
London N1 9PF

Publisher: Sarah Bloxham
Writer: Caroline Smith
Managing Editor: Samantha Warrington
Project Editor: Miranda Harrison
Assistant Editor: Jo Morley
Design: Blanche Williams at Harper Williams Ltd.
Patterns: Bil-Kon Computer Company
Pattern layout design: Stephen Dew
Photography: Paul Michael Hughes; Simon Pask
Production: Rohana Yusof

ISBN: 9781906417840

A catalogue record for this book is available from the British Library.

Printed in China by 1010 Printing International Ltd.

Contents

How to use this book

All the information you will need on how to make the Bold & Beautiful clothes is found in chapter 1. Step-by-step instructions show you how to construct each garment, along with helpful guides on fabric amounts, laying out the patterns and what sewing skills are needed. A complete beginner should start with the simple tunic. Instructions on how to make the optional pockets are at the end of the chapter. In chapter 2 you will find an outline of the techniques used, while chapter 3 gives you the patterns for one size – see chart opposite. On the CD you will find a full range of sizes.

Fabric amounts

The amount of material you need to buy for the project is indicated here, plus any additional items needed.

Layout diagram

This shows the best placing of the pattern pieces on the fabric, prior to cutting out. A larger version accompanies the patterns.

Skills needed

Techniques needed for the project are listed here, with a reference to the full explanation in chapter 2.

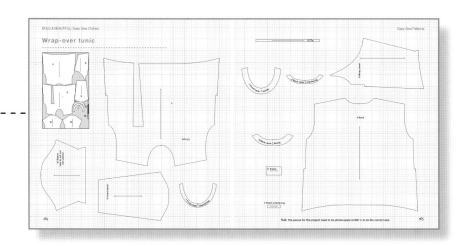

Pattern pieces

These pages give you the option to scale up or photocopy your chosen pattern in the size given. Alternatively, a full range of sizes, easy to print off on A4 paper, is supplied on the CD.

Pockets
The Bold & Beautiful clothes can be made with or without pockets; instructions for these are found in their own section.

Illustrations
Photographs illustrate any of the trickier steps in the garment construction.

Sizing chart
This chart shows you the single dress size per garment for the pattern pieces given in chapter 3. As the garments in this book are not tightly fitted, the dress sizes are therefore given as a size range. Some of the garments are more loosely fitting than others, and so for these the corresponding size range is wider.

	UK dress size	Making the garment	Pattern pieces
Simple tunic	14–20	pp.10–13	pp.98–99
Hankie-hem tunic	12–30	pp.14–17	pp.100–101
Asymmetric tunic	12–30	pp.18–21	pp.102–103
Wrap-over tunic	20–26	pp.22–25	pp.104–105
Tucked dress or tunic	12–30	pp.26–29	pp.106–107
Asymmetric dress	20–22	pp.30–33	pp.108–109
Pinafore dress	16–18	pp.30–33	pp.110–111
Side-buttoned jacket	20–22	pp.38–41	pp.112–113
Waistcoat	20–30	pp.42–45	pp.114–115
Kimono jacket	20–30	pp.46–49	pp.116–117
Yoked jacket	12–22	pp.50–53	pp.118–119
Buttoned coat	12–22	pp.54–57	pp.120–121
Gathered skirt	16–18	pp.58–61	pp.122–123
Harem pants	16–18	pp.62–65	p.124
Wide-leg trousers	20–22	pp.66–69	p.125

1

MAKING THE BOLD & BEAUTIFUL CLOTHES

In this chapter you will find out how to make the Bold & Beautiful clothes. Step-by-step instructions will lead you through the process of constructing each garment, from the first seams right through to the last detail.

Simple tunic

This short-sleeved tunic is simplicity itself to make, and the white linen fabric is the ideal choice for a summer top. Team the tunic with a long-sleeved T-shirt or sweater in cooler weather and get the most out of this versatile garment.

The side seams of the tunic are not stitched right down to the hem edge. Instead they are left open to form side slits.

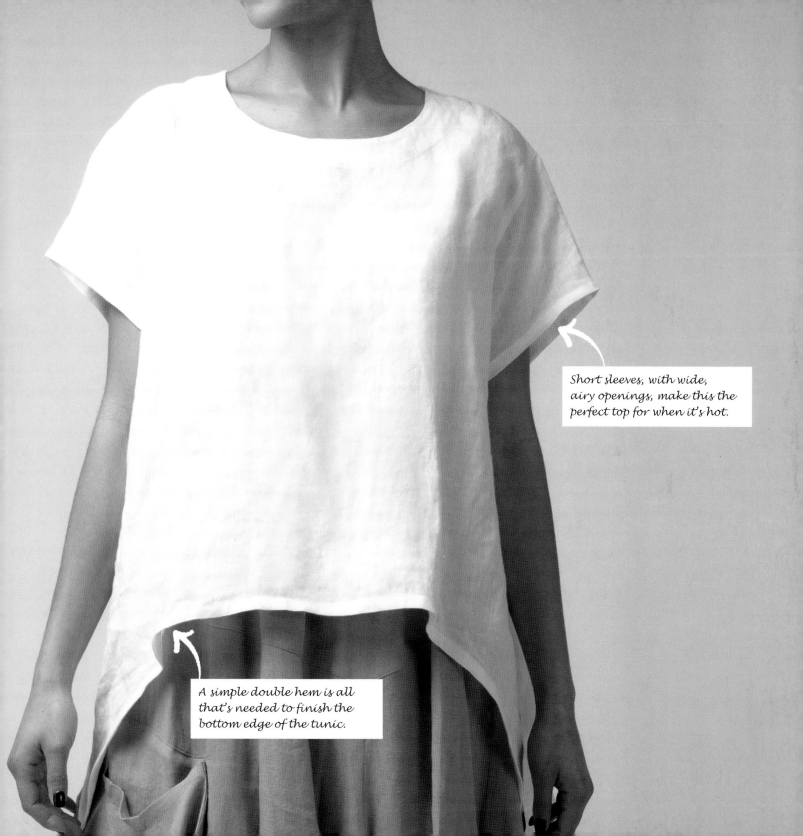

Short sleeves, with wide, airy openings, make this the perfect top for when it's hot.

A simple double hem is all that's needed to finish the bottom edge of the tunic.

Making the simple tunic

You will need

Fabric:
140.5cm of 140cm-wide linen
Lightweight fusible interfacing

Pattern (see p.98):

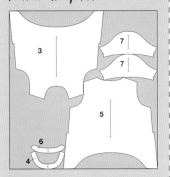

Skills:
Basic seams and hems p.84
Finishing seams p.86
Facings p.88
Interfacing p.88

Before you start Using the simple tunic layout diagram (see p.98) and the pattern pieces, cut out all the pieces of fabric required, making sure you cut on the correct grain line. Transfer any marks from the pattern to the fabric. Cut out pieces of interfacing using the front- and back-neck interfacing pieces. Fuse the interfacing to all the relevant fabric pieces.

1 Pin the front- and back-neck facing pieces right sides together at the shoulder seams; stitch. Press the seams open. Turn under the hem of the longer (outer) edge of the **facing**, and then tack and press.

2 Pin the front and back pieces right sides together at the **shoulder seams**; stitch. Finish the raw edges. Press the shoulder seams towards the back; topstitch.

3 Pin the neck facing to the body at the **neckline**, right sides together and matching the notches and shoulder seams; stitch. Finish the raw edges along the seam.

4 Turn the facing under to the wrong side of the garment; press. Topstitch around the neckline, close to the edge, then topstitch around the turned and pressed edge of the facing.

5 Turn under 1cm hems on both **sleeve cuffs**; press. Turn the hems under again by 1.5cm; pin and press. Pin each sleeve to the armhole, right sides together, matching the notch at the top of the sleeve to the shoulder seam; stitch. Finish the raw edges. Press the seams towards the body; topstitch along these seams.

6 Fold the garment so the front and back are right sides together, and pin along the side and sleeve seams, making sure the armhole seams meet at the underarm. Starting at the underarm, stitch the sleeves' seams.

7 Starting at the underarm again, stitch the **side seams** taking a 1.5cm seam allowance; stop stitching at the first notch along the seam. Finish the raw edges of the stitched side and underarm seams. Snip into the seam allowances at the end of the stitching and press the side and underarm seams towards the back; topstitch these seams.

8 Fold under the raw edge at the **slits** by 1cm; press. Fold under again by 1.5cm; press. Topstitch all round the slits.

9 Turn under 1cm **hems** along the bottom edge of both front and back; press. Turn the hems under again by 1.5cm. Pin and press; then topstitch in place. Topstitch the pressed sleeve hems.

Hankie-hem tunic

The unusual hemline of this tunic gives the garment an interesting silhouette. The points of the hem flare out as you move to create a shape that flatters any figure. Pleats are used to add structure and detail.

Both the back and front of the tunic are made up of an upper and lower section, joined by a horizontal seam.

Pleats are folded into the fabric and then stitched in place. This changes the way the fabric falls and drapes over the body.

The back of this garment has added interest with pleats being used to give some shape to the lower section.

The neckline of the tunic is gently scooped and finished with a simple facing.

A deeply curving bottom edge and long side slits give the tunic its distinctive 'hankie-hem' finish.

Making the hankie-hem tunic

You will need

Fabric:
210cm of 140cm-wide linen
Lightweight, fusible interfacing

Pattern (see p.100):

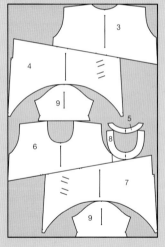

Skills:
Basic seams and hems p.84
Finishing seams p.86
Facings p.88
Interfacing p.88
Darts p.90

Before you start Using the hankie-hem tunic layout diagram (see p.100) and the pattern pieces, cut out all the pieces of fabric required, making sure you cut on the correct grain line. Transfer any marks from the pattern to the fabric. Cut out pieces of interfacing using the front- and back-neck interfacing pieces. Fuse the interfacing to all the relevant fabric pieces.

1 Take the **lower front** section and pin the marked **darts** on the right side; stitch and press. Repeat to stitch the darts on the **lower back** section.

2 Pin the top edge of the lower front to the bottom edge of the **upper front**, right sides together; stitch. Finish the raw edges of the seam and press it towards the top; topstitch. Repeat to stitch the lower back to the **upper back**.

3 Pin the front- and back-neck **facing** pieces right sides together at the shoulder seams; stitch. Press the seams open. Turn under the hem of the longer (outer) edge of the facing; tack and press.

4 Pin the front and back pieces right sides together at the **shoulder seams**; stitch. Finish the raw edges. Press the shoulder seams towards the back; topstitch.

5 Pin the neck facing to the body at the **neckline**, right sides together and matching the notches and shoulder seams; stitch. Finish the raw edges along the seam.

6 Turn the facing under to the wrong side of the garment; press. Topstitch around the neckline, close to the edge, then topstitch around the turned and pressed edge of the facing.

7 Turn under 1cm hems on both **sleeve cuffs**; press. Turn the hems under again by 1.5cm; pin and press. Pin each sleeve to the armhole, right sides together, matching the notch at the top of the sleeve to the shoulder seam; stitch. Finish the raw edges. Press the seams towards the body; topstitch along these seams.

8 Fold the garment so the front and back are right sides together, and pin along the side and sleeve seams, making sure the armhole seams meet at the underarm. Starting at the underarm, stitch the sleeves' seams.

9 Starting at the underarm again, stitch the **side seams** taking a 1.5cm seam allowance. On the left seam, stop stitching at the first notch along the seam. On the right seam, stop stitching at the horizontal seam across the front and back. Finish the raw edges of the stitched side and underarm seams. Snip into the seam allowances at the end of the stitching and press the side and underarm seams towards the back; topstitch these seams.

10 Fold under the raw edge at the **slits** by 1cm; press. Fold under again by 1.5cm; press. Topstitch all round the slits.

11 Turn under 1cm **hems** along the bottom edge of both front and back; press. Turn the hems under again by 1.5cm. Pin and press; then topstitch in place. Topstitch the pressed sleeve hems.

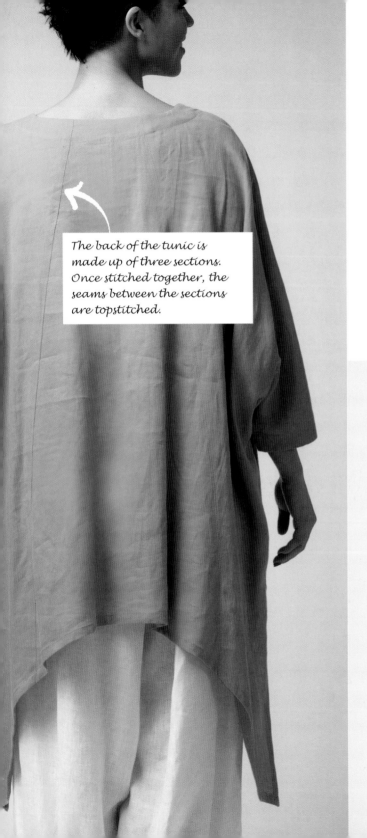

The back of the tunic is made up of three sections. Once stitched together, the seams between the sections are topstitched.

Asymmetric tunic

A gathered panel, set into the lower front of one side of this tunic, creates an attractive design detail. The interesting, asymmetric styling of the tunic is achieved by adding a simple pocket opposite the gathered panel.

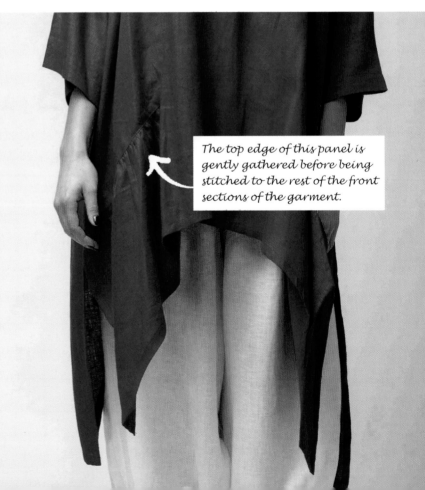

The top edge of this panel is gently gathered before being stitched to the rest of the front sections of the garment.

The pocket can be placed on
either side of the garment -
right or left - with the
gathered panel set on the
opposite side.

The simple pocket that's used
with this garment is stitched
into the front sections along
the top edge only.

Making the asymmetric tunic

Before you start Using the asymmetric tunic layout diagram (see p.102) and the pattern pieces, cut out all the pieces of fabric required, making sure you cut on the correct grain line. Transfer any marks from the pattern to the fabric. Cut out pieces of interfacing using the front- and back-neck interfacing pieces. Fuse the interfacing to all the relevant fabric pieces.

You will need

Fabric:
208cm of 140cm-wide linen
Lightweight fusible interfacing

Pattern (see p.102):

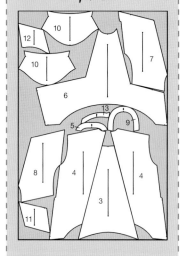

Skills:
Basic seams and hems p.84
Finishing seams p.86
Facings p.88
Interfacing p.88
Gathering p.90

1 The **centre front** is shaped like an upside-down T. Lay the centre front out flat and mark the top edge of the left-hand side of the 'T bar'. Gather up this edge until it measures the same as the bottom edge of the **left front**. Secure the gathering thread. Pin the gathered edge to the bottom edge of the left front, right sides together; stitch. Finish the raw edges of the seam and press upwards; topstitch along this seam.

2 Make up the asymmetric pocket (see p.72), if using, without turning under the top edge of the pocket back. Pin the top edge of the pocket back to the top edge of the right-hand side of the 'T-bar', centring the pocket on that edge and matching raw edges. Tack in place. Pin this edge, with the pocket tacked to it, to the bottom edge of the **right front**, right sides together; stitch. Finish the raw edges of the seam and press upwards; topstitch along this seam. (If not using the pocket, simply stitch the right-hand side of the 'T-bar' to the right front.)

3 Bring the **left front** and centre front right sides together; pin and stitch. Finish the raw edges of the seam and press towards the side; topstitch along this seam. Repeat to pin and stitch the **right front** to the centre front.

4 Pin the **left back** to the centre back, right sides together; stitch. Finish the raw edges of the seam and press towards the side; topstitch along this seam. Repeat to stitch the **right back** to the centre back.

5 Pin the front- and back-neck **facing** pieces right sides together at the shoulder seams; stitch. Press the seams open. Turn under the hem of the longer (outer) edge of the facing; tack and press.

6 Pin the front and back pieces right sides together at the **shoulder seams**; stitch. Finish the raw edges. Press the shoulder seams towards the back; topstitch.

7 Pin the neck facing to the body at the **neckline**, right sides together and matching the notches and shoulder seams; stitch. Finish the raw edges along the seam.

8 Turn the facing under to the wrong side of the garment; press. Topstitch around the neckline, close to the edge, then topstitch around the turned and pressed edge of the facing.

9 Turn under 1cm hems on both **sleeve cuffs**; press. Turn the hems under again by 1.5cm; pin and press. Pin each sleeve to the armhole, right sides together, matching the notch at the top of the sleeve to the shoulder seam; stitch. Finish the raw edges. Press the seams towards the body; topstitch along these seams.

10 Fold the garment so the front and back are right sides together, and pin along the side and sleeve seams, making sure the armhole seams meet at the underarm. Starting at the underarm, stitch the sleeves' seams.

11 Starting at the underarm again, stitch the **side seams** taking a 1.5cm seam allowance; stop stitching at the first notch along the seam. Finish the raw edges of the stitched side and underarm seams. Snip into the seam allowances at the end of the stitching and press the side and underarm seams towards the back; topstitch these seams.

12 Fold under the raw edge at the **slits** by 1cm; press. Fold under again by 1.5cm; press. Topstitch all round the slits.

13 Turn under 1cm **hems** along the bottom edge of both front and back; press. Turn the hems under again by 1.5cm. Pin and press then topstitch in place. Topstitch the pressed sleeve hems.

Sewing Secrets

For this version of the tunic, the gathered panel is featured on the left with the asymmetric pocket on the right. If wished, you can swap these and have the gathered panel on the right and the pocket on the left.

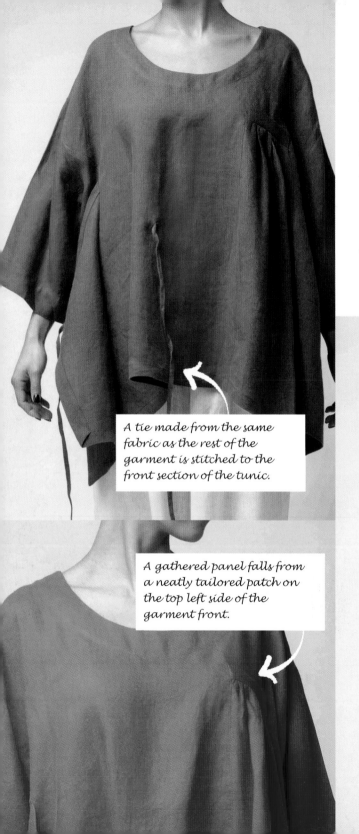

Wrap-over tunic

The eye-catching feature of this tunic is the wrap-over panel. Inserted in the side seam, the panel drapes across the body to be held in place with a fabric tie. A gathered section on the opposite side adds extra interest.

A tie made from the same fabric as the rest of the garment is stitched to the front section of the tunic.

A gathered panel falls from a neatly tailored patch on the top left side of the garment front.

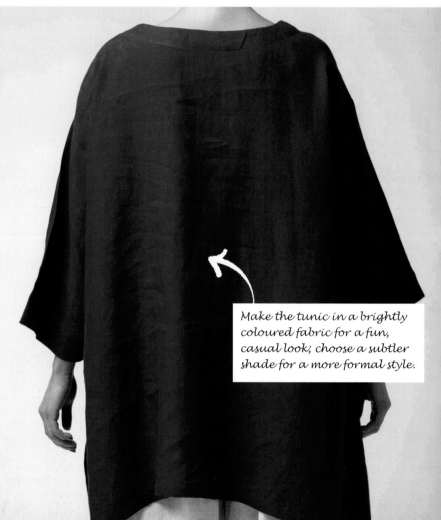

Make the tunic in a brightly coloured fabric for a fun, casual look; choose a subtler shade for a more formal style.

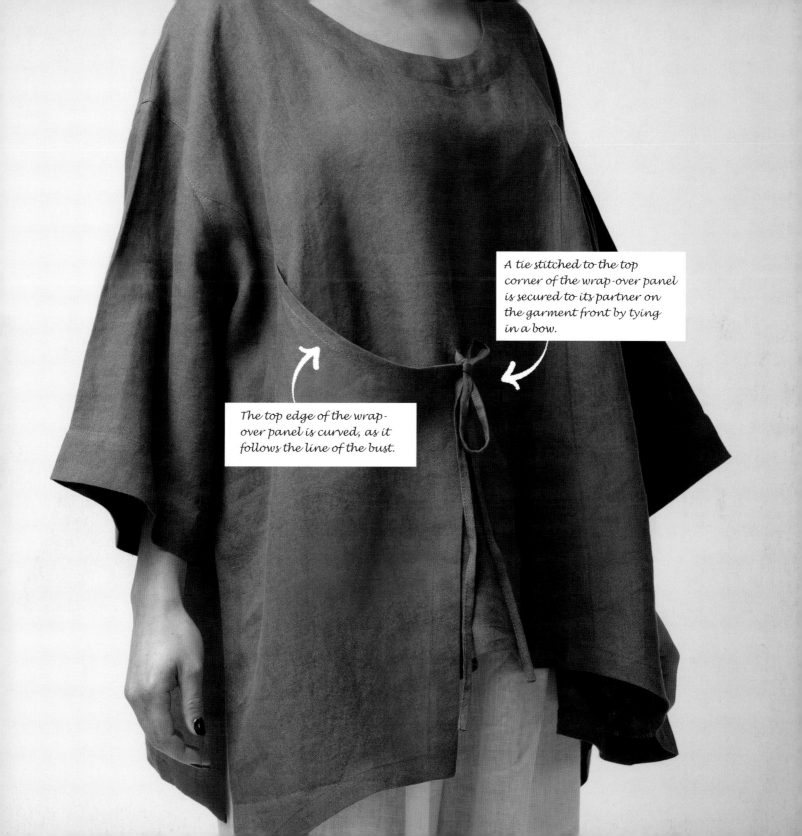

A tie stitched to the top corner of the wrap-over panel is secured to its partner on the garment front by tying in a bow.

The top edge of the wrap-over panel is curved, as it follows the line of the bust.

Making the wrap-over tunic

Before you start Using the wrap-over tunic layout diagram (see p.104) and the pattern pieces, cut out all the pieces of fabric required, making sure you cut on the correct grain line. Transfer any marks from the pattern to the fabric. Cut out pieces of interfacing using the front- and back-neck and patch interfacing pieces. Fuse the interfacing to all the relevant fabric pieces.

1 Take the **patch** piece and fold in half lengthways, right sides together. Stitch along the short ends. Trim the allowance and snip across the corners. Turn to the right side; press. Finish the raw edges. Make up the two ties as described on p.92.

2 Take the **insert panel** and gather up the top edge (see p.90) until it measures about 16cm. There should be 1.5cm of ungathered fabric on either side of the gathering.

3 The insert panel is stitched into the rectangular opening on the main front piece. To do this, pin the top edge of the rectangular opening to the top, gathered edge of the insert panel, matching the raw edges. Adjust the gathers to fit. Then pin the sides of the rectangular opening to the sides of the insert panel, matching raw edges. Stitch all round the edges of the insert panel.

4 Finish the raw edges of the seam and press outwards, away from the insert panel. Topstitch down the sides of the rectangular opening on the right side of the garment. Take the patch piece and pin it at the top of the insert panel on the right side, so the folded edge is topmost and overlapping the pressed seam at the top of the insert panel; stitch. Fold the patch upwards and press. Topstitch along the sides and bottom edge of the patch.

5 Take the **wrap panel** and lay it out flat, wrong side up. Turn under the sloping edge and straight edges on the left by 1cm; press. Turn under again by 1.5cm, securing the end of one **tie** under the hem in the corner between the two turned edges. Topstitch all round, making sure you stitch the tie down.

6 Take the main **front** and lay it out flat, right side up. Place the wrap panel on top, right side up, matching the raw edges at the underarm and side seam. Pin together at the curved underarm seam and stitch.

7 Lay the front and wrap panel out flat again, right side up. Mark the point where the corner of the wrap panel touches the main front. Stitch the remaining **tie** in this position.

8 Pin the front- and back-neck **facing** pieces right sides together at the shoulder seams; stitch. Press the seams open. Turn under the hem of the longer (outer) edge of the facing; tack and press.

9 Pin the front and back pieces right sides together at the shoulder seams; stitch. Finish the raw edges. Press the shoulder seams towards the back; and topstitch.

10 Pin the neck facing to the body at the **neckline**, right sides together and matching the notches and shoulder seams; stitch. Finish the raw edges along the seam.

11 Turn the facing under to the wrong side of the garment; press. Topstitch around the neckline, close to the edge, then topstitch around the turned and pressed edge of the facing.

12 Turn under 1cm hems on both **sleeve cuffs**; press. Turn the hems under again by 1.5cm; pin and press. Pin each sleeve to the armhole, right sides together, matching the notch at the top of the sleeve to the shoulder seam; stitch. Finish the raw edges. Press the seams towards the body; topstitch along these seams.

13 Fold the garment so the front and back are right sides together, and pin along the side and sleeve seams, making sure the armhole seams meet at the underarm. Starting at the underarm, stitch the sleeves' seams.

14 Starting at the underarm again, stitch the **side seams** taking a 1.5cm seam allowance; stop stitching at the first notch along the seam. Finish the raw edges of the stitched side and underarm seams. Snip into the seam allowances at the end of the stitching and press the side and underarm seams towards the back; topstitch these seams.

15 Fold under the raw edge at the **slits** by 1cm; press. Fold under again by 1.5cm; press. Topstitch all round the slits.

16 Turn under 1cm **hems** along the bottom edge of both front and back; press. Turn the hems under again by 1.5cm. Pin and press then topstitch in place. Topstitch the pressed sleeve hems.

Tucked dress or tunic

This Bold & Beautiful garment can be made in two lengths – as a dress or as a tunic. Crisp tucks in the centre front and back gather up the fabric to fit. The tuck feature is repeated on the garment pocket.

Tucks are used to gather up the fabric at the top of the garment. At the bottom of the tucks the excess fabric forms soft folds.

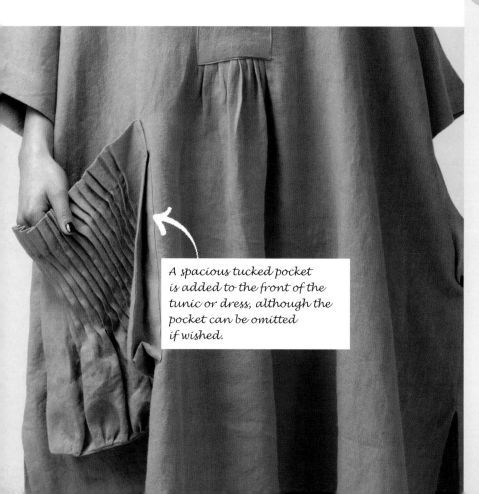

A spacious tucked pocket is added to the front of the tunic or dress, although the pocket can be omitted if wished.

A neat and simple patch of fabric is stitched over the bottom of the tucks to add interest and to help hold them in place.

Sugary shades are an ideal fabric choice for this softly feminine dress or tunic.

Slit openings in the bottom of the side seams give the tunic a flaring outline and a charming, swinging silhouette.

You will need

Fabric:
286cm of 140cm-wide linen
Lightweight fusible interfacing

Pattern (see p.106):

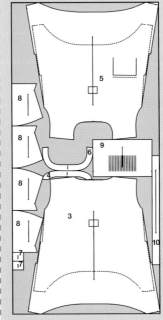

Skills:
Basic seams and hems p.84
Finishing seams p.86
Facings p.88
Interfacing p.88
Tucks p.91

Making the tucked dress or tunic

Before you start Using the tucked dress layout diagram (see p.106) and the pattern pieces, cut out all the pieces of fabric required, making sure you cut on the correct grain line. If you are making the tunic option, cut out the shorter version of the front and back pieces (indicated on the pattern by the dotted line). Transfer any marks from the pattern to the fabric. Cut out pieces of interfacing using the front- and back-neck interfacing pieces. Fuse the interfacing to all the relevant fabric pieces.

1 Pin the front- and back-neck **facing** pieces right sides together at the shoulder seams; stitch. Press the seams open. Turn under the hem of the longer (outer) edge of the facing; tack and press.

2 Pin the front and back pieces right sides together at the **shoulder seams**; stitch. Finish the raw edges. Press the shoulder seams towards the back; topstitch.

3 Pin the neck facing to the body at the **neckline**, right sides together and matching the notches and shoulder seams; stitch. Finish the raw edges along the seam.

4 Turn the facing under to the wrong side of the garment; press. Topstitch around the neckline, close to the edge, then topstitch around the turned and pressed edge of the facing.

5 Take the two **patch** pieces and turn under the raw edges by 5mm, trimming away the excess at the corners. Press and tack all round. Set aside.

6 Starting at the centre, and working outwards, fold 11 blind **tucks** into the **front**, each tuck taking up 1cm of fabric (see p.91) and 49cm long. Press well. Topstitch each tuck in place, starting your stitching just below the edge of the facing; do not topstitch the tucks on the facing section. Repeat to make the same number of tucks on the **back**.

7 Pin one of the patches at the bottom of the front tucks, wrong side of the patch to right side of the front. Topstitch all round the patch, close to the folded edge. Repeat to stitch the remaining patch at the bottom of the tucks on the back. If using, make up the **tucked pocket** and stitch in place on the front as described on p.73.

8 Pin together two **sleeve** pieces along the straight edge; stitch. Finish the raw edges and press the seam open. Repeat with the remaining sleeve pieces.

9 Turn under 1cm hems on both **sleeve cuffs**; press. Turn the hems under again by 1.5cm; pin and press. Pin each sleeve to the armhole, right sides together, matching the notch at the top of the sleeve to the shoulder seam; stitch. Finish the raw edges. Press the seams towards the body; topstitch along these seams.

10 Fold the garment so the front and back are right sides together, and pin along the side and sleeve seams, making sure the armhole seams meet at the underarm. Starting at the underarm, stitch the sleeves' seams.

11 Starting at the underarm again, stitch the **side seams** taking a 1.5cm seam allowance; stop stitching at the first notch along the seam. Finish the raw edges of the stitched side and underarm seams. Snip into the seam allowances at the end of the stitching and press the side and underarm seams towards the back; topstitch these seams.

12 Fold under the raw edge at the **slits** by 1cm; press. Fold under again by 1.5cm; press. Topstitch all round the slits.

13 Turn under 1cm **hems** along the bottom edge of both front and back; press. Turn the hems under again by 1.5cm. Pin and press then topstitch in place. Topstitch the pressed sleeve hems.

Asymmetric dress

Cunning pleats and a clever use of shaped panels give this dress its unusual and flattering form. Short sleeves and the airy, floaty skirt make this a perfect summer dress. The spacious pocket adds a practical detail.

The asymmetric pleat that gives this dress its style wraps around the waist to finish on the back of the garment.

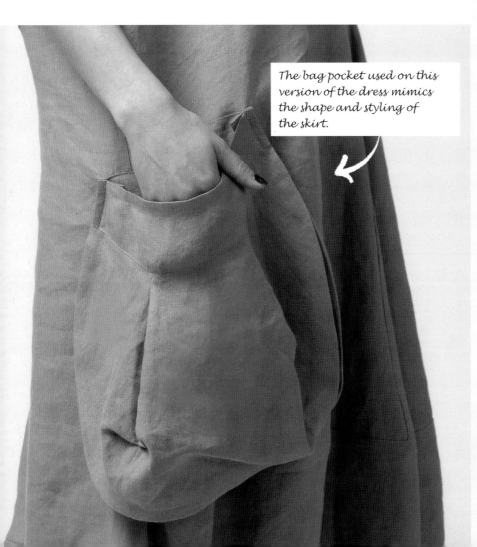

The bag pocket used on this version of the dress mimics the shape and styling of the skirt.

The skirt part of the dress is made up of several sections that are stitched together and then finished with a strip at the hem.

Once the front and back have been constructed, they are sewn together at one side and then the pleat is added.

You will need

Fabric:

293cm of 140cm-wide linen

Lightweight fusible interfacing

Pattern (see p.108):

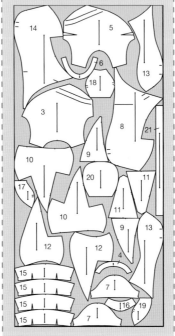

Skills:

Basic seams and hems p.84

Finishing seams p.86

Facings p.88

Interfacing p.88

Darts and tucks pp.90–91

Making the asymmetric dress

Before you start Using the asymmetric dress layout diagram (see p.108) and the pattern pieces, cut out all pieces of fabric required, making sure you cut on the correct grain line as indicated. Transfer any marks from the pattern to the fabric. Cut out pieces of interfacing using the front- and back-neck interfacing pieces. Fuse the interfacing to all the relevant fabric pieces.

1 Take the six **skirt front** pieces (A–F) and pin A to B, B to C, C to D, D to E, E to F, right sides together, matching notches. Stitch. Press the seams to one side. Repeat to stitch together the six **skirt back** pieces.

2 Fold and pin the bust **darts** on the top front piece; stitch and press. Pin the assembled skirt front section to the **top front** piece, right sides together and matching notches; stitch. Finish the raw edges and press the seam upwards; topstitch. Stitch the skirt back to the **top back** in the same way.

3 Pin the front- and back-neck **facing** pieces right sides together at the shoulder seams; stitch. Press the seams open. Turn under the hem of the longer (outer) edge of the facing; tack and press.

4 Pin the front and back pieces right sides together at the **shoulder seams**; stitch. Finish the raw edges. Press the shoulder seams towards the back; topstitch.

5 Pin the neck facing to the body at the **neckline**, right sides together and matching the notches and shoulder seams; stitch. Finish the raw edges along the seam.

6 Turn the facing under to the wrong side of the garment; press. Topstitch around the neckline, close to the edge, then topstitch around the turned and pressed edge of the facing.

7 Turn under 1cm hems on both **sleeve cuffs**; press. Turn the hems under again by 1.5cm; pin and press. Pin each sleeve to the armhole, right sides together, matching the notch at the top of the sleeve to the shoulder seam; stitch. Finish the raw edges. Press the seams towards the body; topstitch along these seams.

8 Fold the garment so the front and back are right sides together, and pin the left side and sleeve seams, making sure the armhole seams meet at the underarm. Starting at the underarm, stitch the **sleeve seam**. Starting at the underarm again, stitch the **side seam**. Finish the raw edges and press the seam towards the back; topstitch. Turn the garment to the right side.

9 Following the guidelines on the pattern, fold in place the **asymmetric tuck** that runs around from front to back. Press and stitch in place. If using, make up the **bag pocket** and stitch in place as described on p.75.

10 Fold the garment back to the wrong side again and pin and stitch the right side and sleeve **seams**, following the method described in step 8.

11 Fold and pin the **darts** in the hem strips; stitch and press. Pin the short ends of the hem strips right sides together; stitch. Press the seams to one side. Turn up a double **hem** all round one long edge; press and stitch.

12 Pin the **hem strip** to the bottom of the dress, right sides together and matching raw edges. Stitch and press the seam towards the top; topstitch all round. Topstitch the pressed sleeve hems.

Sewing Secrets

If wished, the hem strip (see step 11) could be cut on the bias (see p.83). When cutting on the bias you use more fabric, but you get more stretch in the hem. You may wish to use the same technique in other Bold & Beautiful garments that use a hem strip (see pp. 36, 60).

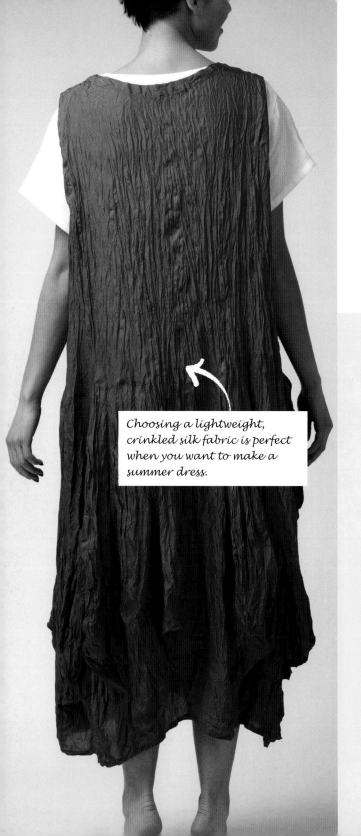

Pinafore dress

Every wardrobe needs a versatile dress that can be worn over several seasons; this pinafore dress fits the bill. On its own, it's the ideal option for hot-weather days. Wear it over warmer clothes for spring or autumn.

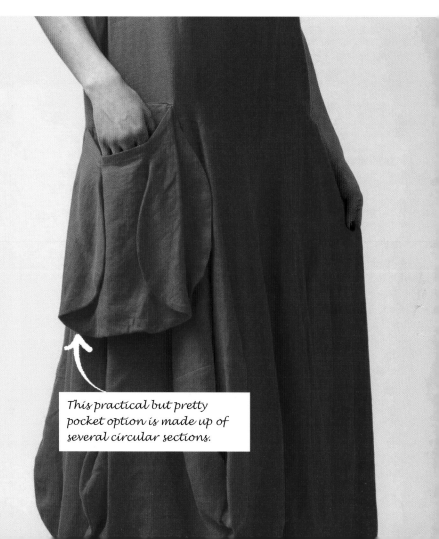

Choosing a lightweight, crinkled silk fabric is perfect when you want to make a summer dress.

This practical but pretty pocket option is made up of several circular sections.

The armholes of this sleeve-less dress are neatly finished with facings that are top-stitched in place all round.

The hem of this dress is finished with a separate strip of fabric that's stitched around the bottom edge of the skirt.

You will need

Fabric:
364cm of 140cm-wide linen
Lightweight fusible interfacing

Pattern (see p.110):

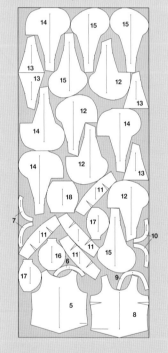

Skills:
Basic seams and hems p.84
Finishing seams p.86
Facings p.88
Interfacing p.88
Darts p.90

Making the pinafore dress

Before you start Using the pinafore dress layout diagram (see p.110) and the pattern pieces, cut out all the pieces of fabric required, making sure you cut on the correct grain line. Transfer any marks from the pattern to the fabric. Cut out pieces of interfacing using the front- and back-neck, and front- and back-armhole, interfacing pieces. Fuse the interfacing to all the relevant fabric pieces.

1 Take the eight **skirt front** pieces (A–H) and pin A to B, B to C, C to D, D to E, E to F, F to G, G to H, right sides together, matching notches. Stitch. Press the seams to one side. Repeat to stitch together the eight **skirt back** pieces.

2 Fold and pin the bust **darts** on the top front piece; stitch and press. Pin the assembled skirt front section to the bottom edge of the **top front** piece, right sides together and matching notches; stitch. Finish the raw edges and press the seam upwards; topstitch. Stitch the skirt back to the **top back** in the same way.

3 Pin the front- and back-neck **facing** pieces right sides together at the shoulder seams; stitch. Press the seams open. Turn under the hem of the longer (outer) edge of the facing; tack and press.

4 Pin the front and back pieces right sides together at the **shoulder seams**; stitch. Finish the raw edges. Press the shoulder seams towards the back; topstitch.

5 Pin the neck facing to the body at the **neckline**, right sides together and matching the notches and shoulder seams; stitch. Finish the raw edges.

6 Turn the facing under to the wrong side of the garment; press. Topstitch around the neckline, close to the edge, then topstitch around the turned and pressed edge of the facing.

7 Take one front-**armhole facing** piece and pin it to one back-armhole facing piece at the shoulder seam, right sides together. Stitch and press the seam open. Repeat with the remaining armhole facing pieces.

8 Pin the armhole facings to the **armholes**, right sides together; stitch. Turn under the raw edges by 1cm; press. Do not turn the facings to the inside of the garment.

9 Fold the garment so the front and back are right sides together, and pin along the right side seam and along the right armhole-facing seam, making sure the **armhole seams** meet at the underarm. Starting at the underarm, stitch the armhole facing seam. Starting at the underarm again, stitch the **side seam**. Finish the raw edges and press the seam towards the back.

10 Turn the armhole facing under so it's on the wrong side of the garment; press. Topstitch along the side seam and then around the armhole, close to the edge. Topstitch around the armhole again, around the turned and pressed edge of the facing.

11 If using, make up the **circle pocket** and stitch in place as described on p.74. Fold the garment back to the wrong side again and pin and stitch the left side and armhole-facing **seams**, following the method described in step 9.

12 Fold and pin the **darts** in the hem strips; stitch and press. Pin the short ends of the hem strips right sides together; stitch. Press the seams to one side. Turn up a double **hem** all round one long edge; press and stitch.

13 Pin the assembled **hem strip** to the bottom of the dress, right sides together and matching raw edges. Stitch and press the seam towards the top; topstitch all round.

The unusual collar detail at the jacket's neck appears on both front and back of the garment.

Side-buttoned jacket

This smart jacket has just enough tailoring to really give it the edge. The shaped front opening, positioned to one side, creates an interesting, asymmetric outline. An unusual collar detail enhances the flattering scooped neckline.

A distinctive half-mandarin collar is used at one side of the neckline of this jacket.

Simple ties on the back allow you to gently gather the jacket in to fit your shape.

Large, mother-of-pearl buttons draw attention to the unusual front opening and are a stylish decorative detail.

Making the side-buttoned jacket

You will need

Fabric:
188cm of 140cm-wide linen
Lightweight fusible interfacing
4 buttons

Pattern (see p.112):

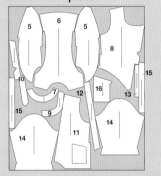

Skills:
Basic seams and hems p.84
Finishing seams p.86
Facings p.88
Interfacing p.88
Ties p.92
Buttons and buttonholes p.92

Before you start Using the side-buttoned jacket layout diagram (see p.112) and the pattern pieces, cut out all the pieces of fabric required, making sure you cut on the correct grain line. Transfer any marks from the pattern to the fabric. Cut out pieces of interfacing using the left- and right-front interfacing pieces, the right front neck, the back neck and the collar piece. Fuse the interfacing to all the relevant fabric pieces.

1　Take the **collar** piece and fold in half lengthways, right sides together. Stitch along the short ends. Trim the seam allowance and snip across the corners. Turn to the right side; press. Make up the two **ties** as described on p.92.

2　Pin a tie to the centre **back** section at the notch marked on the right side seam, matching raw edges; tack. Then tack the remaining tie at the opposite mark on the centre back. Pin the left back section to the centre back section, right sides together and matching notches. Stitch the seam, taking a 1.5cm seam allowance; stop stitching at the first notch along the seam. Repeat to stitch the right back section to the centre back. Finish the raw edges. Snip into the seam allowances at the end of the stitching and press the seams towards the sides; topstitch.

3　Fold under the raw edges at the **slits** by 1cm; press. Fold under again by 1.5cm; press. Topstitch all round the slits. Turn under the bottom hem of the centre back section by 1cm; press. Turn under again by 1.5cm and topstitch in place.

4　Pin the front- and back-neck **facing** pieces right sides together at the right shoulder seam, matching notches; stitch and press the seam open. Pin the left-front facing to the back-neck facing, right sides together, at the left shoulder seam; stitch and press the seam open. Pin the right-front facing to the front-neck facing, right sides together and matching notches; stitch and press the seam open. Turn under the hem of the outer (longer) edge of the assembled facing; tack and press.

5　Pin the left front to the assembled back piece (see step 2), right sides together at the left **shoulder**; stitch. Repeat to stitch the right front to the back at the right shoulder. Finish the raw edges. Press the shoulder seams towards the back; topstitch.

6 Pin the collar piece to the **neckline** at the marked position – it will start on the front and end on the back; tack in place. Pin the facing to the neckline and openings, right sides together and matching notches; stitch. Snip off any points and corners on the right facing to reduce bulk.

7 Turn the facing under to the wrong side of the garment; press. Topstitch around the neckline, close to the edge, then topstitch along the turned and pressed edge of the right-front facing. Topstitch around the turned and pressed edge of the neck facing, starting at the line of topstitching along the right opening and carrying on all round the front neck, back neck, and down the left-front facing.

8 If using, make up the **box-pleat pocket** and stitch in place on the left front as described on p.76.

9 Turn under 1cm hems on both **sleeve cuffs**; press. Turn the hems under again by 1.5cm; pin and press. Pin each sleeve to the armhole, right sides together, matching the notch at the top of the sleeve to the shoulder seam; stitch. Finish the raw edges. Press the seams towards the body; topstitch along these seams.

10 Fold the garment so the front and back are right sides together, and pin along the side and sleeve seams, making sure the armhole seams meet at the underarm. Starting at the underarm, stitch the sleeves' seams. Starting at the underarm again, stitch the **side seams** taking a 1.5cm seam allowance; stop at the first notch along the seam. Finish the raw edges of the stitched side and underarm seams. Snip into the seam allowances at the end of the stitching and press the side and underarm seams towards the back; topstitch these seams.

11 Fold under the raw edge at the **slit** by 1cm; press. Fold under again by 1.5cm; press. Topstitch all round the slit.

12 Turn under 1cm **hems** along the bottom edges of both front and back; press. Turn the hems under again by 1.5cm. Pin and press then topstitch in place. Topstitch the pressed sleeve hems.

13 Make **buttonholes** along the right front opening. Sew buttons in corresponding positions on the left front opening.

Waistcoat

This waistcoat is the ideal piece for mixing and matching. Team it with both short- and long-sleeved garments when you need an extra layer.

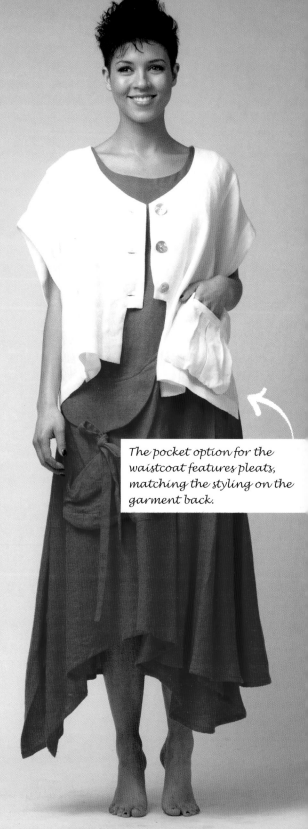

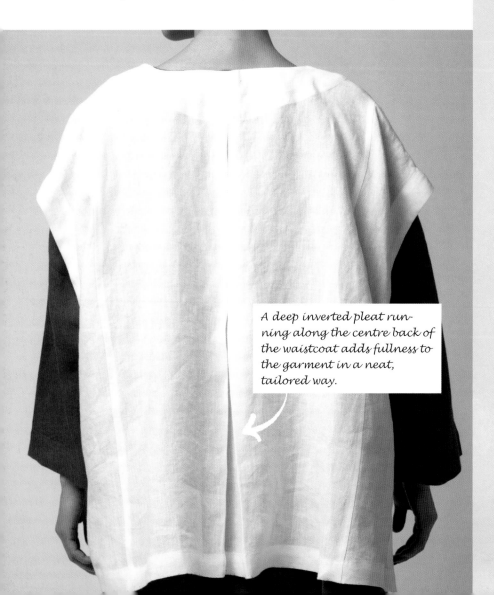

A deep inverted pleat running along the centre back of the waistcoat adds fullness to the garment in a neat, tailored way.

The pocket option for the waistcoat features pleats, matching the styling on the garment back.

Although the waistcoat is sleeveless, the wide profile at the shoulders gives the appearance of cap sleeves.

The shaped edges of the front facings give the waistcoat real visual interest when the garment is buttoned up.

Making the waistcoat

You will need

Fabric:
146cm of 140cm-wide linen
Lightweight fusible interfacing
3 buttons

Pattern (see p.114):

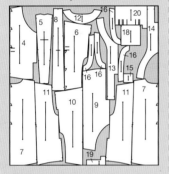

Skills:
Basic seams and hems p.84
Finishing seams p.86
Facings p.88
Interfacing p.88
Pleats p.91
Buttons and buttonholes p.92

Before you start Using the waistcoat layout diagram (see p.114) and the pattern pieces, cut out all the pieces of fabric required, making sure you cut on the correct grain line. Transfer any marks from the pattern to the fabric and cut the buttonhole template from paper only. Cut out pieces of interfacing using the left- and right-front, front- and back-armhole, and the back-neck interfacing pieces. Fuse the interfacing to all the relevant fabric pieces.

1 Take the **patch** piece and turn under the raw edges by 5mm, trimming away the excess at the corners. Press and tack all round. Set aside.

2 Take the three **right front** pieces (A–C); pin piece A to piece B, right sides together and matching notches. Pin piece C to piece B, right sides together and matching notches. Stitch the seams, finish the raw edges, and press towards the sides. Topstitch along the seams. Bring the topstitched edges together on the right side, so the panel between them is folded into an inverted pleat. Press and tack to hold in place. Place the patch at the marked position on top of the pleat, on the right side, and pin in place. Topstitch all round the patch, close to the fold.

3 Take the three **centre back** pieces (D–F) and stitch together in the same way as described in step 2, joining D to E, then F to E. Finish the seams and create a central inverted pleat in the same way. Topstitch triangle shapes on the inverted pleat in the positions marked, to hold the pleat in place.

4 Take the two **left front** pieces (G and H) and pin right sides together, matching notches; stitch. Finish the raw edges and press the seam towards the side; topstitch. If using, make up the **pleated pocket** and stitch in place as described on p.74.

5 Take the **left back** piece and pin to the assembled centre back (see step 3), right sides together and matching notches; stitch. Finish the raw edges and press the seam towards the side; topstitch. Repeat to stitch the **right back** piece to the centre back.

6 Pin the left-front and right-front **facings** to the back-neck facing. Stitch and then press the seams open. Turn under the hem of the longer (outer) edge of the facing; tack and press.

7 Pin the front to the back at the **shoulder seams**, right sides together; stitch. Finish the raw edges. Press the seams towards the back; topstitch.

8 Pin the facing around the **neckline** and along the front openings, right sides together. Stitch along the front opening edges, around the neckline and along the hem edges. Turn the facing under to the wrong side of the garment; press. Topstitch around the neckline and opening, close to the edge, then topstitch around the turned and pressed edge of the facing.

9 Take one front-**armhole facing** piece and pin it to one back-armhole facing piece at the shoulder seam, right sides together. Stitch and press the seam open. Repeat with the remaining front- and back-armhole facing pieces. Pin the armhole facings to the armholes, right sides together; stitch. Turn under the raw edges by 1cm; press. Do not turn the facings to the inside of the garment.

10 Fold the garment so the front and back are right sides together, and pin along the side seams and along the armhole facing seams, making sure the armhole seams meet at the underarm. Starting at the underarm, stitch the armhole facing seam.

11 Starting at the underarm again, stitch the **side seams** taking a 1.5cm seam allowance; stop stitching at the first notch along the seam. Finish the raw edges of the stitched side and armhole-facing seams. Snip into the seam allowances at the end of the stitching and press the side and armhole-facing seams towards the back; topstitch these seams. Fold under the raw edge at the slits by 1cm; press. Fold under again by 1.5cm; press. Topstitch all round the slits.

12 Turn the armhole facing under to the wrong side; press. Topstitch all round the **armhole**, then topstitch around the turned and pressed edge of the facing.

13 Turn under a 1cm **hem** on both front and back; press. Turn the hems under again by 1.5cm. Pin and press then topstitch in place. Make **buttonholes** along the right front opening using the buttonhole paper template as a guide. Sew buttons in corresponding positions on the left front opening.

Kimono jacket

Sometimes you need a jacket that you can simply throw over anything. This jacket is perfect; combine it with loose-fitting tunics and dresses for a casual look, or with plain-coloured tops and trousers for smart day wear.

The back of the jacket features a deep slit, perfect if you wish to reveal a glimpse of the garments worn underneath.

Wide, full-length sleeves mean that you can wear this jacket with any number of tops, from short sleeved to long.

The jacket opening is held closed with a single button; a mother-of-pearl button adds a decorative touch.

The right-front opening is finished with a wide, almost triangular facing.

Making the kimono jacket

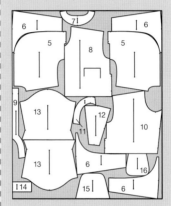
Before you start Using the kimono jacket layout diagram (see p.116) and the pattern pieces, cut out all the pieces of fabric required, making sure you cut on the correct grain line. Transfer any marks from the pattern to the fabric. Cut out pieces of interfacing using the placket, right front- and back-neck and the left-front interfacing pieces. Fuse the interfacing to all the relevant fabric pieces.

1 To make up the **lower-back** section, take two of the lower-back pieces and pin, right sides together, along the centre-back notched edge. Stitch along the seam from the point at the top up to the notch. Snip into the seam allowance at the end of the stitching. Press the seam open. Finish the curved raw edge at the top. Repeat with the remaining two lower-back pieces.

2 Pin the two assembled lower-back sections right sides together, along the bottom edge and up the sides of the centre slit; stitch. Turn to the right side and press. Topstitch along the bottom edge and around the slit.

3 Pin the left **back** to the right back, right sides together along the centre seam; stitch up to the notch. Finish the raw edge of the seam and then press it towards one side; topstitch. Finish the bottom raw edge.

4 Pin the assembled lower-back section to the bottom edge of the back, right sides together and matching the centre seams on both parts; stitch. Press the seam towards the top and then topstitch all round.

5 Pin the front- and back-neck **facing** pieces right sides together at the right shoulder seam, matching notches; stitch and press the seam open. Pin the left-front facing to the back-neck facing, right sides together, at the left shoulder seam; stitch and press the seam open. Turn under the hem of the longer (outer) edge of the assembled facing; tack and press.

6 If using, make up the **patch pocket** and stitch in place on the left **front** as described on p.76. Pin the left front to the assembled back piece, right sides together at the left **shoulder**; stitch. Repeat to stitch the right front to the back at the right shoulder. Finish the raw edges. Press the seams towards the back; topstitch.

7 Pin the facing to the **neckline** and left-front opening, right sides together and matching notches; stitch. Snip into the curve of the seam allowance around the neckline. Turn the facing under to the wrong side of the garment; press. Topstitch around the neckline and opening, close to the edge, then topstitch again around the turned and pressed edge of the facing.

8 Take the **placket** and turn under the two long edges by 1cm; press. Fold the placket in half lengthways, right sides together, and stitch along the two short edges. Turn to the right side and press.

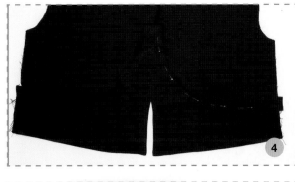

9 Turn under a 1cm hem on the bottom edge of the right front and turn again by 1.5cm; press. Take the placket and slip it onto the right front, so that the raw edge at the front opening is enclosed by the placket. Pin along the turned edge, and then topstitch in place, making sure you stitch through all the layers.

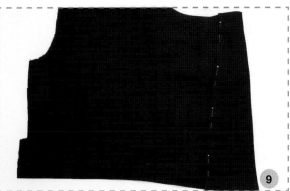

10 Turn under 1cm hems on both **sleeve cuffs**; press. Turn the hems under again by 1.5cm; pin and press. Pin each sleeve to the armhole, right sides together, matching the notch at the top of the sleeve to the shoulder seam; stitch. Finish the raw edges. Press the seams towards the body; topstitch along these seams.

11 Fold the garment so the front and back are right sides together, and pin along the side and sleeve seams, making sure the armhole seams meet at the underarm. Starting at the underarm, stitch the sleeves' seams.

12 Starting at the underarm again, stitch the **side seams** taking a 1.5cm seam allowance; stop stitching at the first notch along the seam. Finish the raw edges of the stitched side and underarm seams. Snip into the seam allowances at the end of the stitching and press the side and underarm seams towards the back; topstitch these seams.

13 Fold under the raw edges at the **slits** by 1cm; press. Fold under again by 1.5cm; press. Topstitch all round the slits.

14 Turn under 1cm **hems** along the bottom edge of left front; press. Turn under a 1cm hem. Pin and press. Topstitch along both front bottom edges. Topstitch the pressed sleeve hems. Make a **buttonhole** at the top of the placket, using the buttonhole template as a guide. Sew a button in the corresponding position on the left front opening.

Yoked jacket

Everyone deserves something special in their wardrobe, something that makes them look good and which draws admiring glances whenever it's worn. This jacket, with its stylish details, is just such a garment.

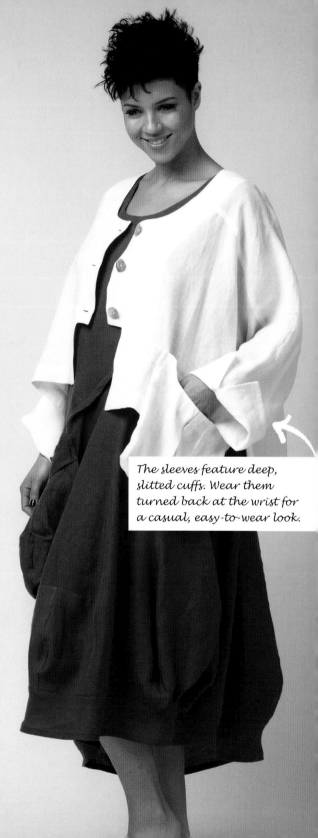

The sleeves feature deep, slitted cuffs. Wear them turned back at the wrist for a casual, easy-to-wear look.

The pleated back of this jacket is finished with a neat patch detail, stitched over the pleat to hold it in place.

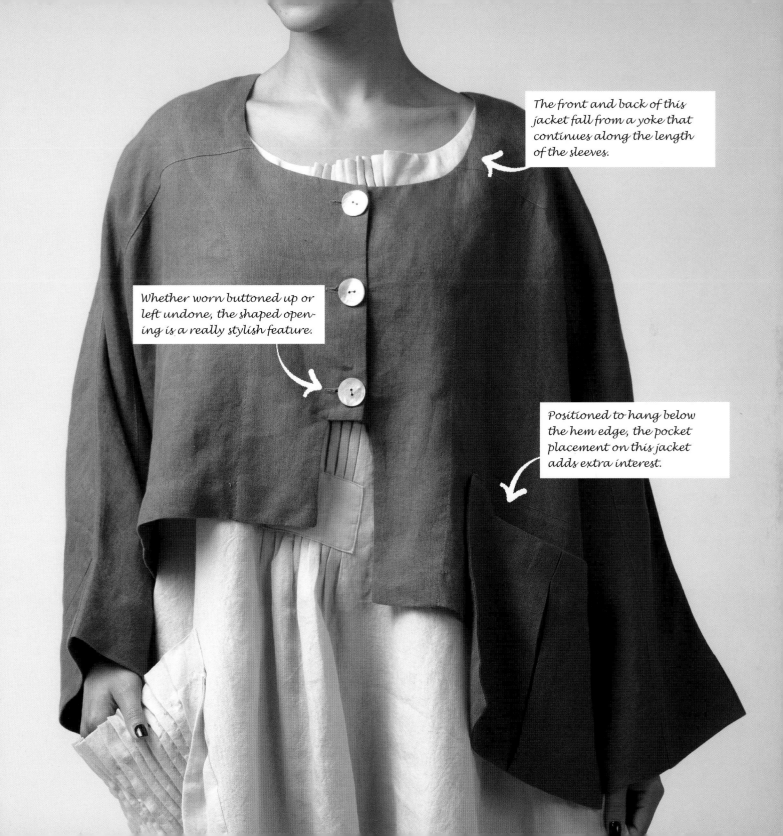

The front and back of this jacket fall from a yoke that continues along the length of the sleeves.

Whether worn buttoned up or left undone, the shaped opening is a really stylish feature.

Positioned to hang below the hem edge, the pocket placement on this jacket adds extra interest.

Making the yoked jacket

Before you start Using the yoked jacket layout diagram (see p.118) and the pattern pieces, cut out all the pieces of fabric required, making sure you cut on the correct grain line. Transfer any marks from the pattern to the fabric and cut the buttonhole template from paper only. Cut out pieces of interfacing using the left- and right-front and the back-neck interfacing pieces. Fuse the interfacing to all the relevant fabric pieces.

1 Take the back **patch** piece and turn under the raw edges by 5mm, trimming away the excess at the corners. Press and tack all round. Set aside.

2 To make the **cuffs**, take two of the cuff pieces and pin, right sides together, along the longer of the sides (the curved edge is the top edge). Stitch from the point at the top up to the notch. Snip into the seam allowance at the end of the stitching. Press the seam open. Repeat with the remaining six cuff pieces so you have four assembled cuff pieces.

3 Open out two of the assembled cuff pieces, and pin right sides together, along the bottom edge and up the sides of the centre slit; stitch. Repeat with the remaining two assembled cuff pieces.

4 Slightly open out one of the cuffs, so the seam just stitched is running along the centre. With the right sides still together, pin the two straight raw edges together. There will be a seam on both sides; pin across the seams, folding them both in the same direction. Stitch. Repeat with the second cuff. Turn both the cuffs to the right side and press. Topstitch around the bottom edge and around the slit on both. Finish the curved raw edges and then turn them under by 1.5cm; press. Set aside.

5 On the **back** there are five evenly spaced notches along the top edge (the centre notch lines up with the centre of the back). Bring in the outer notches to meet the centre notch, to form an inverted pleat (see p.91); pin and press. Tack in place.

6 Position the patch on top of the pleat, on the right side, 15–20cm down from the top edge; pin in place. Topstitch all round the patch, close to the fold.

7 Pin one front **yoke** and one back yoke along the top edge, right sides together; stitch. Press the seam towards the back; topstitch. Repeat to stitch the remaining yoke pieces together. Pin the two back yoke sections right sides together at the centre-back seam. Stitch, press the seam to one side; topstitch.

You will need

Fabric:
161cm of 143cm-wide linen
Lightweight, fusible interfacing
3 buttons

Pattern (see p.118):

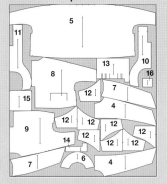

Skills:
Basic seams and hems p.84
Finishing seams p.86
Facings p.88
Interfacing p.88
Pleats p.91
Buttons and buttonholes p.92

8 Pin the bottom edge of of the back yoke to the top edge of the back, right sides together and matching notches; stitch. Press the seam upwards and then topstitch.

9 If using, make up the **pleated pocket** and stitch in place on the left **front** as described on p.74. Pin the bottom edge of the left-front yoke to the top edge of the left front, matching notches. Stitch, press the seam upwards; topstitch. Repeat to stitch the right-front yoke to the top of the right front.

10 Pin the left-front and right-front **facings** to the back-neck facing. Stitch the seams and press open. Turn under the hem of the longer (outer) edge of the facing; tack and press.

11 Pin the facing around the **neckline** and along the front openings, right sides together. Stitch along the front opening edges, around the neckline and along the hem edges. Turn the facing under to the wrong side of the garment; press. Topstitch around the neckline, close to the edge, then topstitch around the turned and pressed edge of the facing.

12 Fold the jacket so the front and back are right sides together and pin the side and underarm **seams**. Stitch, starting at the end of the sleeve. Stop stitching at the first notch along the seam. Finish the raw edges of the seams. Snip into the seam allowances at the end of the stitching and press the seams towards the back; topstitch these seams.

13 Fold under the raw edge at the **slits** by 1cm; press. Fold under again by 1.5cm; press. Topstitch all round the slits.

14 Take one of the cuffs and, with the **sleeve** right side out, slip it onto a sleeve so that the end of the sleeves slips between the two layers of the cuff. Match the slit-seam of the cuff to the seam that runs along the top of the sleeve. Pin and then topstitch around the top edge of the cuff, close to the pressed turning. Repeat with the other cuff.

15 Turn under a 1cm **hem** on both the front and back; press. Turn the hems under again by 1.5cm. Pin and press, and then topstitch in place. Using the buttonhole template as your guide, make a row of buttonholes along the right front.

2

3

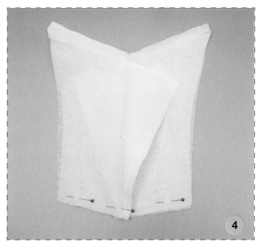

4

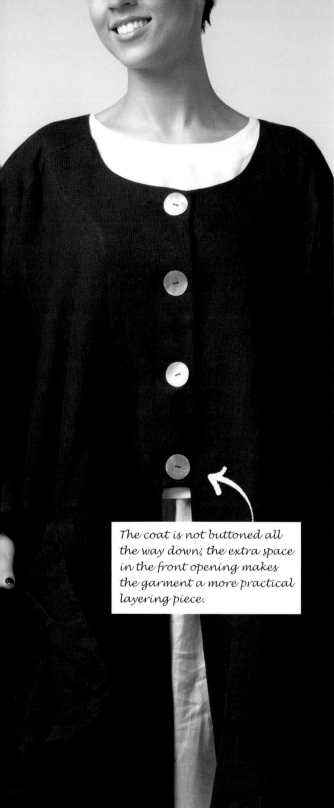

Buttoned coat

A good-quality coat is an essential, especially when you want a longer outer layer to wear with trousers or shorter dresses and skirts. This mid-calf-length coat is just the job; the pleated shaping lets you wear it with almost anything.

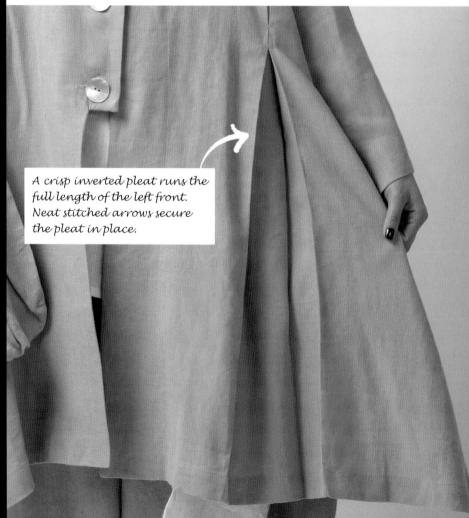

A crisp inverted pleat runs the full length of the left front. Neat stitched arrows secure the pleat in place.

The coat is not buttoned all the way down; the extra space in the front opening makes the garment a more practical layering piece.

The coat back also features inverted pleats, running at an angle from the neckline edge right down to the hem.

The pocket option for the coat is a practical roomy style; ideal for an everyday garment. The pocket can be omitted if wished.

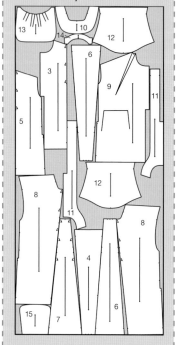
Making the buttoned coat

Before you start Using the buttoned coat layout diagram (see p.120) and the pattern pieces, cut out all the fabric pieces required, making sure you cut on the correct grain line. Transfer any marks from the pattern to the fabric. Cut out pieces of interfacing using the left- and right-front and the back-neck interfacing pieces. Fuse the interfacing to all the relevant fabric pieces.

1 Take the three **left front** pieces (A–C); pin piece A to piece B, right sides together and matching notches. Pin piece C to piece B, right sides together and matching notches. Stitch the seams, finish the raw edges, and press towards the sides. Topstitch along the seams. Bring the topstitched edges together on the right side, so the panel between them is folded into an inverted pleat. Press and topstitch triangle shapes on the inverted pleat in the positions marked, to hold the pleats in place.

2 Take the three **centre back** pieces (D–F) and stitch together in the same way as described in step 1, joining D to E, then F to E. Take the **left back** and pin to the edge of the assembled centre-back section, right sides together; stitch. Repeat to stitch the **right back** to the centre-back section. Finish the seams and create two inverted pleats in the same way as described in step 1. Topstitch triangle shapes on the inverted pleat in the positions marked, to hold the pleats in place.

3 Take the right front and fold the **dart** in position; stitch and press to one side. If using, make up the **big pocket** and stitch in place as described on p.72.

4 Pin the left-front and right-front **facings** to the back-neck facing. Stitch and then press the seams open. Turn under the hem of the longer (outer) edge of the facing; tack and press.

5 Pin the front to the back at the **shoulder seams**, right sides together; stitch. Finish the raw edges. Press the seams towards the back; topstitch.

6 Pin the facing around the **neckline** and along the front openings, right sides together. Stitch along the front opening edges, around the neckline, and along the hem edges. Turn the facing under to the wrong side of the garment; press. Topstitch around the neckline and opening, close to the edge, then topstitch around the turned and pressed edge of the facing.

7 Turn under 1cm hems on both **sleeve cuffs**; press. Turn the hems under again by 1.5cm; pin and press. Pin each sleeve to the armhole, right sides together, matching the notch at the top of the sleeve to the shoulder seam; stitch. Finish the raw edges. Press the seams towards the body; topstitch along these seams.

8 Fold the garment so the front and back are right sides together, and pin along the side and sleeve seams, making sure the armhole seams meet at the underarm. Starting at the underarm, stitch the sleeves' seams.

9 Starting at the underarm again, stitch the **side seams** taking a 1.5cm seam allowance; stop stitching at the first notch along the seam. Finish the raw edges of the stitched side and underarm seams. Snip into the seam allowances at the end of the stitching and press the side and underarm seams towards the back; topstitch these seams.

10 Fold under the raw edge at the **slits** by 1cm; press. Fold under again by 1.5cm; press. Topstitch all round the slits.

11 Turn under 1cm **hems** along the bottom edge of both front and back; press. Turn the hems under again by 1.5cm. Pin and press then topstitch in place. Topstitch the pressed sleeve hems. Make **buttonholes** along the right front opening, using the buttonhole template as a guide. Sew buttons in corresponding positions on the left front opening.

Gathered skirt

When you want to ring the changes, a full-length skirt is a useful option. You can wear it with tighter-fitting sweaters and T-shirts, or team it with looser layers, such as tunics with waistcoats and jackets.

Fullness at the waist is gathered into an elastic waistband, making the skirt easy to put on and take off.

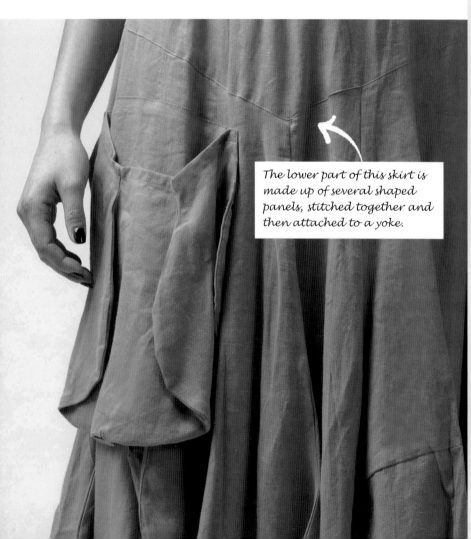

The lower part of this skirt is made up of several shaped panels, stitched together and then attached to a yoke.

The pocket option used here mimics the curved shaping in the skirt sections.

A long strip of fabric is stitched around the bottom edge of the skirt section and then hemmed to finish.

You will need

Fabric:

308cm of 140cm-wide linen

2.5cm-wide elastic to fit comfortably around your waist

Pattern (see p.122):

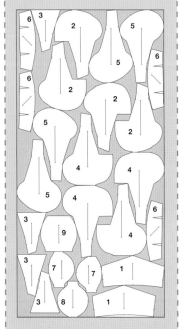

Skills:

Basic seams and hems p.84

Finishing seams p.86

Tucks and darts pp.90–91

Elasticated waists p.93

Making the gathered skirt

Before you start Using the gathered skirt layout diagram (see p.122) and the pattern pieces, cut out all the fabric pieces required, making sure you cut on the correct grain line. Transfer any marks from the pattern to the fabric.

1 Take the eight **skirt front** pieces (A–H) and pin A to B, B to C, C to D, D to E, E to F, F to G, G to H, right sides together, matching notches; stitch. Press the seams to one side. Repeat to stitch together the eight **skirt back** pieces.

2 Fold and pin **tucks** into the bottom of the assembled skirt front and back, as marked on the pattern; stitch and press.

3 Pin the top edge of the skirt front to the bottom edge of the front **yoke**, right sides together; stitch. Finish the raw edges of the seam and press the seam upwards; topstitch. Repeat to stitch the skirt back to the back yoke.

4 Pin the front and back of the skirt right sides together along the **side seams**; stitch. Finish the raw edges of the seam and press open.

5 Turn under the top of the skirt's yoke by 5mm; press. Turn under by a further 2.5cm; pin and press. Topstitch in place, leaving a gap of about 7.5cm in the stitching through which to insert the elastic at step 9.

6 If using, make up the **circle pocket** as described on p.74. Position on the left or right side of the skirt, so the pocket goes over the side seam; pin and stitch in place.

7 Fold and pin the **darts** in the hem strips; stitch and press. Pin the short ends of the hem strips right sides together; stitch. Press the seams to one side. Turn up a double **hem** all round the darted edge; press and stitch.

8 Pin the assembled **hem strip** to the bottom of the skirt, right sides together and matching raw edges. Stitch then finish the raw edges. Press the seam towards the top; topstitch all round.

9 Insert the **elastic** through the gap in the turning at the top of the skirt. Stitch the ends of the elastic together. Topstitch across the opening.

Sewing Secrets

The technique used here for inserting elastic in a waistband is one best suited to the home dressmaker, with a standard sewing machine. A professional seamstress would be more likely to stitch the elastic to the top of the skirt's yoke and then turn the fabric under, stitching the hem down to enclose the elastic and form the waistband. The advantage of this is the elastic will not twist around inside the waistband during wear. The elastic needs to be pulled taut while being sewn. Most domestic sewing machines are not up to piercing the elastic while under tension. However, if you have a top-quality machine, this is a technique you might wish to try.

Harem pants

Trousers are the mainstay of most modern wardrobes – ideal when you're putting together that layered look. From short tunics to longer dresses, you can wear these beautiful harem pants with almost any length of top.

Decorative details feature on both the back and front of these harem pants.

The trousers are elasticated at the waist, for easy wear and making it unnecessary to insert a zip-front closure.

A curved tuck is taken in at the bottom of each trouser leg - on both front and back - to shape and add detail.

Deep, slitted cuffs are stitched to the trouser legs at the ankle, drawing up the fabric for that harem-pant look.

Making the harem pants

- -

You will need

Fabric:
180cm of 140cm-wide linen
Enough 2.5cm-wide elastic to fit comfortably around your waist

Pattern (see p.124):

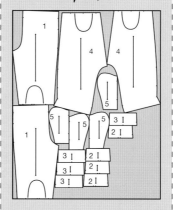

Skills:
Basic seams and hems p.84
Finishing seams p.86
Elasticated waists p.93

Before you start Using the harem pants layout diagram (see p.124) and the pattern pieces, cut out all the pieces of fabric required, making sure you cut on the correct grain line. Transfer any marks from the pattern to the fabric and cut the tuck template from paper only.

1 To make the **cuffs**, take one front and one back cuff and pin right sides together, along the short notched edge. Stitch along the seam to the notch. Snip into the seam allowance at the end of the stitching. Press the seam open. Repeat with the remaining cuff pieces; you now have four assembled cuff pieces.

2 Open out two of the assembled cuff pieces. Pin right sides together, along the bottom edge and up the sides of the centre slit; stitch. Repeat with the remaining two assembled cuff pieces.

3 Take one of the cuffs and open it out slightly, so the seam just stitched is running along the centre. With the right sides still together, pin the two straight raw edges together. There will be a seam on both sides; pin across the seams, folding them both in the same direction. Stitch. Repeat with the second cuff.

4 Turn both the cuffs to the right side and press. Topstitch around the bottom edge and around the slit on both. Turn under raw edges by 1cm; press. Set aside.

5 Take the **leg** pieces and pin the curved tuck in place on each, following marks or using the paper template as a guide. Make sure you fold so you bring the fabric wrong sides together and the tuck is on the right side; stitch.

6 If using, add the **side-seam pocket** to the side seams as instructed on p.77. If not, pin the left front leg to the left back leg along the **side seam**, right sides together; stitch. Finish the raw edges and press the seam open. Repeat to stitch the right front leg to the right back leg.

7 Bring the assembled right and left legs right sides together and pin along the front **crotch seam**; stitch. Pin along the back crotch seam; stitch. Finish the raw edges of the seam and press to one side; topstitch.

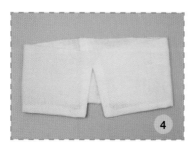

8 Pin along the **inside leg** seams, making sure the front and back crotch seams match. Starting at the crotch, stitch each seam.Trim away any bulk at the point where the inside leg seams meet the crotch seams. Finish the raw edges and press the seams open.

9 On the left leg, fold the bottom of the leg into a **pleat** at the side seam; the bottom of the leg needs to fit into the cuff so you will have to adjust the size of the pleat until it fits. Once you have the pleat right, topstitch it in place for about 3cm. Repeat with the right leg.

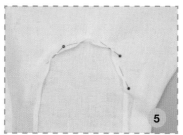

10 Slip the **cuffs** over the ends of the trouser legs; pin in place. Try the trousers on to make sure that each leg is the same length. Topstitch all round the cuffs to stitch to the trousers.

11 Turn under the top of the trousers by 5mm, press. Turn under by a further 2.5cm; pin and press. Topstitch in place, leaving a gap of about 7.5cm in the stitching through which to insert the elastic (see p.93). Insert the **elastic** through the gap and stitch the ends of the elastic together. Topstitch across the opening.

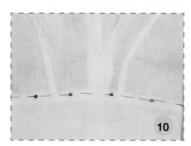

Wide-leg trousers

Although they may be among the most practical garments you'll ever own, trousers don't have to be boring. With a few simple details, it's possible to add an interesting twist to this classic wardrobe staple.

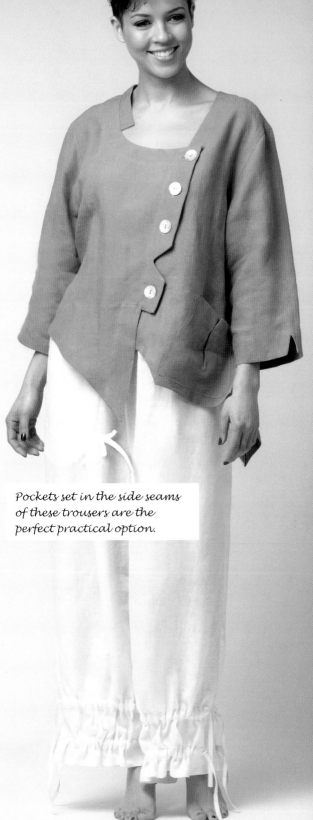

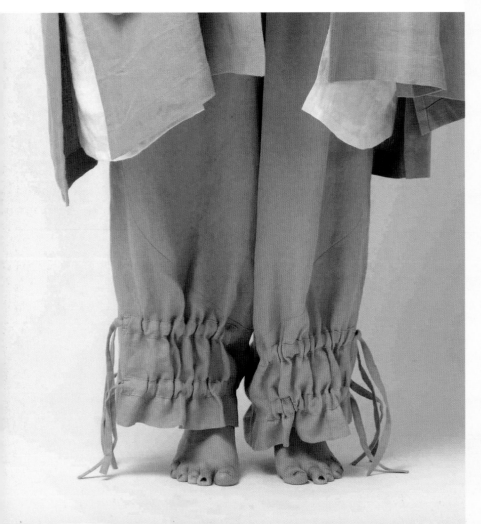

Pockets set in the side seams of these trousers are the perfect practical option.

The ends of the trouser legs are gathered up with ties, stitched into separate casings.

Because the gathered detail is created with the use of separate casings, you may wish to omit this feature and simply have plain legs.

You will need

Fabric:
229cm of 140cm-wide linen
Enough 2.5cm-wide elastic to fit comfortably around your waist

Pattern (see p.125):

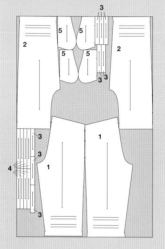

Skills:
Basic seams and hems p.84
Finishing seams p.86
Elasticated waists p.93
Ties p.92

Making the wide-leg trousers

Before you start Using the wide-leg trouser layout diagram (see p.125) and the pattern pieces, cut out all the fabric pieces required, making sure you cut on the correct grain line. Transfer any marks from the pattern to the fabric.

1 Make up the eight **ties** as described on p.92. Take each of the **casing** pieces and turn under all the raw edges by 5mm; press. Set ties and casings aside.

2 If using, add the **side-seam pocket** to the side seams as instructed on p.77. If not, pin the left front leg to the left back leg along the **side seam**, right sides together; stitch. Finish the raw edges and press the seam towards the back; topstitch. Repeat to stitch the right front leg to the right back leg.

3 Turn under the **hem** on each leg by 5mm; press. Turn under again by 1.5cm; press and topstitch in place.

4 Lay one leg section out flat and pin a **casing piece**, wrong side down, at the bottom of the leg, at the position indicated on the pattern. Topstitch along the top of the casing. Insert a tie in the casing, so the raw edge of the tie is tucked in the fold at the short end of the casing furthest from the side seam. The tie should protrude from the casing at the end nearest the side seam.

5 Fold the casing down over the tie and topstitch along the short end furthest from the side seam and along the bottom edge. Make sure you only stitch through the tie at the short end of the casing. Do not topstitch the short end nearest to the side seam.

6 Repeat steps 4 and 5 to stitch another casing and tie above the first as indicated on the pattern. Then stitch two more casings and ties on the other side of the side seam, making sure that the ties protrude from the end of the casing nearest the side seam. Sew the remaining four casings and ties to the other trouser leg in the same way.

7 Bring the assembled right and left legs right sides together and pin along the front **crotch seam**; stitch. Pin along the back crotch seam; stitch. Finish the raw edges of the seam and press to one side; topstitch.

8 Pin along the **inside leg** seams, making sure the front and back crotch seams match. Starting at the crotch, stitch each seam. Trim away any bulk at the point where the inside leg seams meet the crotch seams. Finish the raw edges and press the seams open.

9 Turn under the top of the trousers by 5mm, press. Turn under by a further 2.5cm; pin and press. Topstitch in place, leaving a gap of about 7.5cm in the stitching through which to insert the elastic (see p.93). Insert the **elastic** through the gap and stitch the ends of the elastic together. Topstitch across the opening.

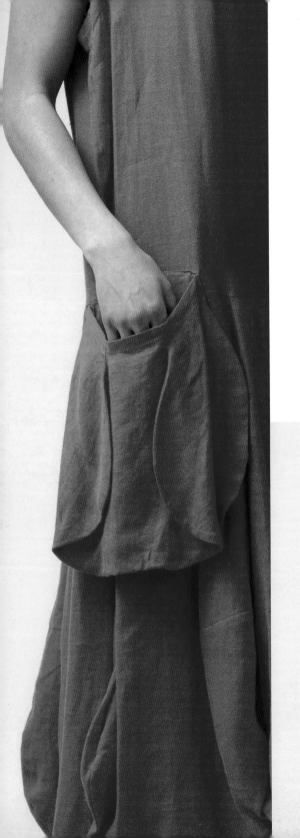

Pockets

Stylish pockets are among the key features of the Bold & Beautiful clothes. Since almost all of the pockets used are stitched directly onto the garment fronts, it is always possible to omit them from the finished item. Even the pockets inserted in side seams can be left out if wished. However, they all add an extra design element to the clothes and, as with all pockets, are immensely practical.

Asymmetric pocket

Before you start Cut out the pocket pieces (see pp.102–103) from your fabric. Finish the raw edges on both pieces.

1 Turn under the top edge of the pocket **front** by 5mm; press. Turn under again by 1cm; pin and press. Topstitch in place.

2 Turn under the top edge of the pocket **back** to the wrong side by 1cm; press. Pin the right side of the pocket front to the wrong side of the pocket back; **stitch** around the sides and bottom edge. Turn the pocket right side out and press. Topstitch round the sides and bottom.

3 Pin the pocket to the garment along the top turned edge; topstitch in place. For the Asymmetric Tunic (see p.20) the pocket is stitched into a seam on the garment front.

Big pocket

Before you start Cut out the pocket pieces (see pp.120–121) from your fabric and use the pocket facing pattern to cut out a piece of interfacing; fuse the interfacing to the pocket facing.

1 Fold the four **darts** as indicated on the right side of the pocket front. Stitch in place. Press the two innermost darts towards the sides; press the two outermost darts in towards the centre. **Gather** up the bottom edge of the pocket front until it is the same length as the bottom edge of the pocket back.

2 Pin the **facing** to the pocket **front**, matching the top edge of the facing to the top edge of the pocket front, right sides together; stitch. Turn under the remaining long raw edge of the facing by 1cm; press. Turn the facing under to the wrong side; press. Topstitch along the turned long edge of the facing, close to the fold.

3 Finish the raw edges on both pocket front and pocket **back**. Turn the top edge of the pocket back to the wrong side by 1cm; press. Pin the right side of the pocket front to the wrong side of the pocket back; **stitch** around the curved edges. Turn the pocket right side out and press. Pin the pocket at the marked position on the garment; topstitch in place along the top, turned edge of the pocket back. Topstitch again along the sides of the faced section of the pocket front.

Tucked pocket

Before you start Cut out the pocket pieces (see pp.106–107) from your fabric. Finish the raw edges on both pieces.

1 Turn under the top edge of the pocket front by 1cm; pin and press. Turn under by a further 4cm; pin and press. Topstitch along the hem edge, close to the fold. Starting at the centre, and working outwards, fold 17 **blind tucks** into the pocket front, each tuck taking up 1cm of fabric (see p.91). Press well.

2 Topstitch each tuck in place, starting your stitching just below the topstitching on the hem edge and stitching for about 15cm; do not topstitch the tucks on the hem turning. **Gather** up the bottom edge of the pocket so that the width of the bottom edge is the same as the width of the top, faced edge.

3 Take the **gusset strip** and turn under the raw short edges by 1cm; press. Turn under again by 1.5cm; press. Pin the gusset strip around the edge of the pocket front, right sides together. Stitch and then finish the raw edges of the seam.

4 Finish the remaining raw edge of the gusset and turn under by 1cm; press. Pin to the garment front in the marked position. Topstitch all round the turned edge of the gusset, close to the fold. Fold the gusset into a pleat at the top on both sides of the pocket, then topstitch down the sides of the pocket for the depth of the facing, to hold the pleat in place.

Circle pocket

Before you start Cut out the pocket pieces (see pp.110–111; pp.122–123) from fabric.

1 Pin one pocket **side** to the outside edge of the pocket **front**, right sides together; stitch. Repeat to stitch the second pocket side to the pocket front. Finish the raw edges of the seams. Press the seams from the right side. Fold the curved sections so they face in, towards each other.

2 Turn under the top edge of the assembled pieces by 5mm; press. Turn under the top edge again by 1cm; pin and topstitch in place.

3 Finish the raw edges on both pocket **front** and pocket **back**. Turn under the top edge of the pocket back to the wrong side by 1cm; press. Pin the right side of the pocket front to the wrong side of the pocket back; stitch around the curved edges. Turn the pocket right side out and press. Pin the pocket at the marked position on the garment front; topstitch in place along the top (turned) edge of the pocket back.

Pleated pocket

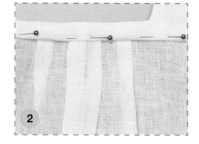

Before you start Cut out the pocket pieces (see pp.114–115; pp.118–119) from your fabric and use the pocket-facing pattern to cut out a piece of interfacing; fuse the interfacing to the pocket facing.

1 Take the pocket front and fold an **inverted pleat** at the centre as marked on the pattern. Fold a single pleat to the left of this, and another to the right as marked on the pattern. Press the pleats and then topstitch along each to hold in place. Gather up the bottom edge of the pocket front until the pocket front is the same width as the pocket back.

2 Pin the pocket **facing** to the pocket front, right sides together; stitch. Turn the facing under to the wrong side. Turn under the raw edge of the facing; pin and press. Topstitch along this edge.

3 Finish the raw edges of the pocket **front** and **back**. Turn the top edge of the pocket back to the wrong side by 1cm; press. Pin the right side of the pocket front to the wrong side of the pocket back; stitch around the side and bottom edges. Turn the pocket right side out; press. Pin to the garment front in the marked position and topstitch in place along the top (turned) edge of the pocket back.

Bag pocket

Before you start Cut out the pocket pieces (see pp.103–104) from your fabric and use the pocket facing pattern to cut out a piece of interfacing; fuse the interfacing to the pocket facing.

1 Take one pocket **side** and pin to the outside edge of the pocket **front**, right sides together; stitch. Repeat to stitch the second pocket side to the pocket front. Finish the raw edges of the seams.

2 Turn under the top edge of the pocket facing by 5mm; press. Turn under the top edge again by 1cm; pin and topstitch in place.

3 Pin the **facing** to the pocket front, matching the top edge of the pocket front to the long raw edge of the facing, right sides together. Stitch and then finish the raw edges of the seam. Press the seam upwards and topstitch in place.

4 Take the **gusset** strip and turn under the short ends by 1cm; press. Turn under again by 1.5cm; press. Pin the gusset strip around the curved edge of the pocket **front**, right sides together. Stitch and then finish the raw edges of the seam.

5 Finish the top raw edge of the pocket **back** and turn it to the wrong side by 1cm; press. Pin the pocket back to the gusset, with the wrong side of the pocket back facing the right side of the gusset and matching raw edges. Stitch and then finish the raw edges of the seam.

6 Turn the pocket right side out and press. Pin it in the marked position on the garment front and topstitch in place along the top (turned) edge of the pocket back. Fold the gusset into a pleat at the top on both sides of the pocket, then topstitch down the sides of the pocket for the depth of the facing, to hold the pleat in place.

Patch pocket

- -

Before you start Cut out the pocket pieces (see pp.116–117) from your fabric and use the pocket facing pattern to cut out a piece of interfacing; fuse the interfacing to the pocket back.

1 Take the pocket front; **gather** up the top edge until it measures 18cm.

2 Turn under the top edge of the pocket **facing** by 5mm; press. Turn under the top edge again by 1cm; pin and topstitch in place. Pin the facing to the pocket front, matching the gathered (top) edge of the pocket front to the long raw edge of the facing, right sides together. Stitch and then finish the raw edges of the seam. Press the seam upwards and topstitch in place.

3 Finish the raw edges on both the pocket **front** and pocket **back**. Turn the top edge of the pocket back to the wrong side by 1cm; press. Pin the right side of the pocket front to the wrong side of the pocket back; stitch around the curved edges. Turn the pocket right side out and press. Pin the pocket at the marked position on the garment; topstitch in place along the top, turned edge of the pocket back.

Inverted pleat pocket

- -

Before you start Cut out the pocket pieces (see pp.112–113) from your fabric.

1 Take the **front** pocket piece and turn under the top edge by 1cm; turn under again by 3cm and tack in place before pressing. Fold a small **inverted pleat** (see p.91) in the centre of the top hem, so that the pocket measures 15cm across at the top. Tack the pleat in place. With the wrong side facing upmost, topstitch along the edge of the tacked hem, stitching over the pleat.

2 Finish the raw edges of the pocket and turn under by 1cm. Pin to the garment front at the marked placement and then topstitch around the sides and bottom.

Side-seam pocket

- -

Before you start **Cut out the pocket pieces (see pp.124–125) from your fabric.**

1 **Measure** down from your waist to the point where you would like the pocket to start. Add on 6cm (for the waistband). Take this measurement and mark a point on the side seam of the left front leg this distance from the top. Mark the same point on the other leg pieces.

2 Pin a pocket piece to the left **front leg** so the top of the pocket is level with the marked point, right sides together and matching raw edges. Stitch. Repeat to stitch the remaining pocket pieces to the remaining leg pieces. Finish the raw edges and press the seam on the right side so the pocket piece is pressed to the outside of the trouser leg.

3 Pin the left front leg to the left **back leg**, right sides together, pinning along the **side seam** at the top of the leg, then round the outside of the pocket pieces, and then down the rest of the side seam to the bottom. Repeat to stitch the right front to the right back leg.

4 Snip into the seam allowances above and below the pockets. Press the pockets towards the front of the trousers. Finish all raw edges and press the outside-leg seams open. Continue to sew the trouser legs together as for your chosen project.

EASY-SEW TECHNIQUES

The Bold & Beautiful clothes are made using straightforward dressmaking techniques.
This chapter features all the skills you will need, from sewing simple seams to adding facings and finishes.

The tools of the trade

- -

To make the Bold & Beautiful clothes there are a few pieces of sewing equipment that are essential, as a well as a few handy optional extras.

Sewing Secrets

It is well worth investing in a good-quality pair of dressmaker's shears – look after them well and they will last a lifetime. Make sure you use them only for cutting fabric; never cut paper with them since this will quickly blunt the blade. Set aside a pair of ordinary household scissors especially for cutting out paper patterns.

The most important tool you will need when making your own clothes is a sewing machine. You will need a model that does straight stitching, zigzag stitch, buttonholes and that has a backstitch feature. Fortunately, these functions are standard on most basic machines. All sewing machines work in more-or-less the same way, but it's always worth consulting your machine's manual to make sure you are threading it correctly.

There are various accessories for sewing machines that can come in useful. A straight-stitch foot is essential, and this should come with your basic machine. You will also need the attachment that allows you to create buttonholes; again, this usually comes as standard with a modern sewing machine. A zip foot can be useful, although none of the projects in this book feature a zip closure.

Overlockers

Top-of-the-range sewing machines will offer lots of other features but, generally speaking, these are usually decorative stitch options that are not always needed in basic dressmaking. The only specialist sewing machine that you might consider acquiring is an overlocker (also known as a serger). This machine will sew a seam, finish the raw edge and cut off the excessive

fabric in one go. You can also use an overlocker to simply stitch a seam or just do the finishing. However, you can use the zigzag stitch on a conventional sewing machine to finish the raw edges of seams.

Needles and pins

Although most of the sewing in this book is done with a sewing machine, you will need occasionally to do some hand sewing – this is usually just tacking – and so you should have a few needles in your sewing kit. These should be ordinary dressmaking needles (known as 'sharps') in an average size – size 6 or 7 will be ideal.

Another essential will be pins. As you assemble a garment, pins hold the different pieces together before they are sewn. And you will need to pin the pattern to your fabric before cutting out. Good quality, long, dressmaker's pins are the best for the job. The types with coloured ball-like heads are particularly useful since they are easier to see and to pick up.

Cutting tools

You will also need some cutting tools. Most essential are dressmaker's shears: these special scissors have handles that are angled upwards so that the blade can lie flat as you cut through fabric. A pair of embroidery scissors can come in handy for trimming seams and snipping into small corners, and a seam ripper is useful for unpicking any mistakes. Have a pair of ordinary scissors set aside for cutting out patterns.

Measuring and marking

A tape measure is another vital tool. You will need one to take your own measurements and to assist in cutting out the patterns. It's also needed to check seams, hems and other parts of a garment.

And, finally, you should have some marking tools in your sewing box. When you cut a pattern piece out of your fabric, you need to transfer information on the pattern to the fabric and you'll need something to do this. There are various types of marker available. Most common is tailor's chalk, which comes in flat triangles of chalk or in a pencil form. Also available are fade-away marker pens. The marks made with these fade after about 48 hours, so don't use these if you are going to mark up your fabric and then set it aside for a few days.

Sewing machine basics

When threading your machine, the reel of thread is placed on a spool pin (1) before being passed through the tension guide (2). It is then threaded into the take-up lever (3) and passed through various guides before being threaded through the needle (4). The bobbin is placed in the bobbin case (5). Most modern, basic machines offer a range of stitch options; you can select the stitch type and size using the selector dial (6). The reverse switch (7) allows you to stitch backwards. Although most machines are set up in the same way, always refer to the manufacturer's manual.

Patterns and fabric

The starting point when making clothes is a sewing pattern. Armed with this, and your chosen fabric, you'll be able to create your own hand-made garment.

Before you even begin cutting out your sewing patterns, you need to take some personal measurements. Start by taking your bust, waist and hip measurements; these will help you decide which size of pattern to select (see the Pattern Section). You then need to take your neck-to-waist, leg-length and arm-length measurements; these will help you if you need to lengthen or shorten any pattern pieces.

Take your measurements wearing just underwear, and make sure you wear your usual bra style. It can be tricky to take measurements on your own, so you may need someone to help. To measure around your bust, wrap the tape measure around the fullest area of the bust. Similarly, for the hips, take the measurement at the fullest point around the hips. For the waist, take a length of string and tie it snugly, but not tightly, around the waist. Bend backwards and forwards, and from side to side; where the string settles is your natural waistline. Measure around the waist at this point.

To take your neck-to-waist measurement, measure from the most prominent backbone at the base of your neck down to the string around your waist. For the leg length, measure from the waist string to the ankle; if you plan to make trousers that will be worn with high heels, measure from the waist to the ground. For the

arm length, measure from the point where the top of your arm meets the shoulder – this is the point where the top of a sleeve would sit – to the small bone that protrudes on your wrist.

After taking your measurements, you must measure your pattern pieces and compare the results. If you discover parts of your chosen pattern will be too long or too short for you, you should make alterations to the pattern before cutting out the fabric.

Pattern marks

Once you've decided on which size pattern you will need and have assembled all the different pieces for your chosen garment, you have to transfer some of the marks printed on the pattern onto your fabric. At the edges of the pattern pieces you will notice some small triangles; these marks are called notches and they help you match up the different pieces of a garment as you put it together. For example, you will see notches marked on the top (curved) edge of the sleeve pattern, and notches marked on the armhole edge of the front and back pieces; when you pin the sleeve to the front and back, you simply make sure that the notches on each part line up.

There are a few ways to mark notches. You can make chalk marks in the right place on the edge of the cut-out fabric pieces; the disadvantage to this is that the marks can be easily rubbed away during handling of the fabric. Or you can cut out a little triangle of fabric in the correct place in the seam allowance; the disadvantage here is that you might make too big a cut. Alternatively, you could use a few tacking stitches to mark the position of notches; the problem with this option is that it is hard to be as accurate. Experiment with the methods until you find one that is right for you.

You will also see, on some garments, details such as pleat and dart positions, and pocket placements. Using tailor's chalk or other erasable fabric marker is the best way to mark such features on your fabric. Always transfer any marks to the fabric before you pin and sew the pieces together; you will not be as accurate in your marking once parts of the garment have been assembled.

Fabric grain

Another important mark on your sewing pattern pieces is the grain line. This is a long line with an arrowhead at either end. You have to position this line on the fabric grain before you cut out the piece. If this isn't done properly, the finished garment will not hang correctly.

A woven fabric has two grain lines; the lengthways and crossways grains. The lengthways grain (the warp) runs parallel to the selvage; the crossways grain (the weft) runs perpendicular to the selvage. When you buy a length of cloth, the selvages are the finished, uncut edges.

If you take a piece of fabric and pull it at a 45° angle to the lengthways grain, it will feel stretchy – much more stretchy than if you pull it along either the lengthways or crossways grains. This 45° angle is known as the bias and any pattern piece 'cut on the bias' will have much more stretch to it.

Finding the grain

The lengthways and crossways grains on a piece of woven fabric are at right angles to each other.

Sewing Secrets

To position a pattern correctly on the grain, pin one end of the marked grain line to the fabric. Measure down to the selvage. Position the other end of the grain line so it is the same distance from the selvage and then pin in place. The marked grain line will be parallel to the selvage.

Basic seams and hems

Whenever you sew together pieces of fabric you are creating a seam; whenever you turn up a fabric edge, you are making a hem. These are the fundamentals of garment construction.

Sewing-machine foot guides

The stitching guide lines on the right of your sewing machine needle will help you maintain a neat and even seam.

To make a seam, you simply bring together two, or maybe more, pieces of fabric and stitch through all the layers. The distance between the stitching and the fabric edge is called the seam allowance. Whatever seam allowance is used, it's important to stick to it throughout – unless otherwise stated – or you will find pattern pieces don't match up. Even a small discrepancy can have a surprising effect. For the garments in this book, 1cm seam allowances have been used.

Stitching a seam

When you are going to machine stitch a seam, first raise the sewing-machine foot and the needle. Place the layers of fabric under the foot and lower it to hold the fabric in place.

• On the right of your sewing-machine needle you will see measurements marked. Line up your fabric edge to the correct measurement – this will help you maintain an even seam allowance.

• Position your fabric so as to start stitching close to the top of the seam. Stitch forward

for a short distance and then stop. Depress the reverse switch and stitch backwards to the beginning of the seam again. Release the switch and stitch forwards to the end of the seam.

• At the end of the seam, depress reverse again and stitch backwards and forwards for a bit. Doing this at the beginning and end of a seam will help secure your thread.

Corners and curves

If you have to stitch around a corner, machine stitch up to that point and then stop with the needle still in the fabric – you may have to stitch slowly to do this accurately. Lift up the presser foot and pivot the fabric until the continuation of the seam lines up with the guide lines on your sewing machine.

Stitching a curved seam takes a bit of practice. Start by lining up the fabric edge with the appropriate marking on your sewing machine. Then start to stitch very slowly and, as you stitch, turn the fabric so that the raw edge stays level with the guide line.

Hems

A hem is created when you fold up the raw edge of a piece of fabric so that it is out of sight; when you are instructed to 'turn under' a hem, you have to fold it to the wrong side. If you turn under the fabric once, you create a single hem; if you fold it under twice, then that is a double hem. If you turn under a single hem it is advisable to finish the raw edge of the fabric first, either with an overlocker or by using the zigzag stitch on your sewing machine. When you turn under a double hem then the first turning will be narrower than the second; if the turnings were the same amount, the hem would be too bulky.

• To turn under a hem, first turn it up to the given amount (usually 1cm) and pin in place. Press all round and then remove the pins.

• Turn up the fabric again, to the second given amount and pin again. Machine stitch along the hem on the wrong side, keeping the stitching close to the folded edge of the first turning.

• Start and finish your stitching at a seam, if possible, and don't use the reverse stitch function to secure the stitching, as it will be visible on the right side. Instead, when you have finished stitching, pull on one of the loose threads on the wrong side of the hem so that you pull through a loop of stitching from the right side. Insert the tip of a pin in the loop and pull on it until you draw through the end of the thread to the wrong side. Tie the two ends of the thread together several times to secure. Repeat with the other two thread ends. Once you've finished stitching, press the hem again.

Tricky corners

Occasionally, you may have to turn up a hem that goes around a corner. When this happens, you don't want to leave any untidy edges poking out. Start by folding up the first turning and pressing.

Then fold up the second turning and press that, but not at the corners. Unfold the two turnings and trim away any excess fabric at the corner. Refold the first turning, and then refold the second turning, folding the hem into a diagonal line at the corner. Press well and then stitch.

Finishing seams and pressing

As you piece together the different parts of a garment, there are a few simple sewing techniques you can use to help you get a neat and smart finished result.

Creating neat finishes

Using an overlocker gives you the neatest finish to the raw edge of a seam allowance.

Topstitching a seam leaves a neat finish on the outside of a garment and helps to ensure a seam lies flat.

After you've sewn together pieces of fabric to create a seam, there will still be what are known as 'raw' edges. These are the cut edges of the fabric at the seam allowance. As a rule, it's a good idea to finish these raw edges in some way to prevent them fraying or unravelling. If you are going to press the seam open (see left), finish each raw edge of a seam allowance; if you are going to press the seam to one side, then finish the raw edges together.

Oversewn edges

The most effective way to finish a seam's edges is to use an overlocker (also known as a serger) which oversews the raw edges. If you don't have access to an overlocker then the zigzag stitch on an ordinary sewing machine can be used instead. Zigzag stitch along the seam allowance close to, but not on, the edge and then trim off the excess fabric close to the stitching.

Bound edges

An alternative is to bind the raw edges of a seam. This is more labour intensive but it does give the inside of a garment a very neat and tailored finish. It's particularly useful in coats and jackets, or any garment that is taken on or off frequently.

• To bind a seam, first measure the length of the seam. If you are going to bind the edges of the seam allowance together, then buy this amount of 25mm-wide bias binding, plus a little extra for turnings; if you are going to bind both edges of the allowance, you will need to buy twice this amount.

• Fold the bias binding in half lengthways and press. Bias binding is sold with both the long edges already turned under, so all you need to do is turn under the short ends and press. Then fold the binding over the seam allowance to be finished and pin in place.

• Stitch along the binding, close to the fold on the long edge, stitching through all the layers of fabric.

Trimming seams

Sometimes, especially when sewing together more than two layers of fabric or when sewing round corners, you end up with a bulky seam. To help make a seam lie flat and neat, it may be necessary to trim the seam allowance in some way. At outer corners, you usually need to snip off the point of the fabric. At inner corners and along curved seams, you should snip into the allowance up to, but not touching, the line of stitching. Occasionally, you may need to trim the width of a seam allowance, especially when adding a facing to a garment (see pp.88–89). This is usually only necessary if you are using a thick fabric.

Pressing

Once you have finished the raw edges of a seam, you should press it. Seams are pressed either open or to one side.

• To press a seam open, lay the fabric on the ironing board wrong side up and hold the seam open at one end with your fingertips. Run the tip of the iron up the seam to open it up and then press down with the soleplate to flatten the seam.

• To press a seam to one side, lay the fabric on the ironing board wrong side up and, with one hand holding the seam allowance down facing the desired direction, iron along it. Turn the fabric to the right side and place a pressing cloth (see right) over the seam, press along it again.

Topstitching

After finishing and pressing a seam you may also want to use topstitching to help make the seam lie flat. This also has the advantage of adding a neat decorative finish to the outside of a garment. Topstitching is simply a line of straight machine stitching that is visible on the right side.

• To topstitch a seam that's been pressed open, place the seam in the sewing machine right side up and machine stitch 5–10mm to the right of the seam, so you are stitching through the top layer of fabric and the seam allowance. Turn the seam around and topstitch along the other side of the seam, keeping to the same distance.

• To topstitch a seam that's been pressed to one side, place the fabric in the sewing machine right side up and with the seam allowance to the right. Machine stitch 5–10mm to the right of the seam, so you are stitching through the top layer of fabric and both the seam allowances.

The importance of pressing

It is essential to press seams as you work, rather than leaving this task until the end of your project. With properly pressed seams it is easier to join together neatly the different parts of a garment. And it's not just seams that need pressing; hems, darts, pleats and tucks all benefit from pressing during construction. It's also a good idea to press your pieces of fabric before stitching them together – it will be difficult to get a neat, flat seam if pieces of fabric are crinkled.

To press effectively, select the correct heat setting on the iron for your chosen fabric. Place the fabric on the ironing board and iron over the element that needs pressing. Apply firm pressure and try not to stretch or pull the fabric as this may distort it. If you are ironing on the right side of the garment, cover it with a pressing cloth first. This is a piece of clean cotton (or any fabric that can take a high heat setting) that protects your fabric during pressing. If you don't use a pressing cloth, you may end up with accidental shiny marks or scorch marks on the actual fabric.

Facings

It's not always possible to use a hem to finish the raw edge of a garment – turning under a curved neckline, for example, might be tricky. This is where you need to use a facing.

Tidy finishing

After stitching the facing to the garment piece, snip the corners and understitch (see p.89) outer edges that might roll to the right side.

Turn the facing to the wrong side of the garment and press.

When making a garment and sewing together the various pieces, you will need to finish the remaining raw edges in some way. As a rule, the ends of sleeves and the bottom edges of the front and back of a garment are finished with hems (see p.85). With the neckline and armhole openings (on a sleeveless garment), these edges are usually curved. Because they would be harder to turn up and hem, they are finished with a facing. The front openings on jackets, coats and waistcoats are also finished with a facing, since you need the extra stability this offers. It is also much more effective to make buttonholes in a faced opening.

The purpose of facing

A facing is a separate piece of fabric that is sewn to the edge of the garment piece and then turned underneath, to the wrong side. The facing is cut to match the shape of the edge to which it is being sewn. On a neckline, for example, the facing will be a curved piece of fabric; the inner curved edge of the facing will exactly match the curved edge of the neckline. Facings must be cut on the same grain (see p.83) as the garment piece to which they are being sewn.

Interfacing

The addition of interfacing adds further stability. Interfacing is a special fabric that is ironed onto, or sewn, to your facing piece. The iron-on type is known as fusible interfacing, and its ease of use makes it a popular choice. Interfacing comes in a variety of weights; you need to select the weight that best suits your fabric and needs. For the interfaced areas in the garments in this book, a light- to medium-weight interfacing is used. You need to use the pattern pieces labelled as 'interfacing' to cut out the interfacing for the corresponding fabric pieces.

How to sew a facing and interfacing

First cut out your garment pieces from the fabric, including the facing piece. Then use the facing pattern to cut out your interfacing.

- Place the interfacing piece on top of the facing piece, centred on the wrong side. Carefully place a pressing cloth over the top and iron over the cloth; set the iron to the setting recommended by the interfacing manufacturer.
- Once you have fused the interfacing to the facing, transfer any markings from the paper pattern to the wrong side of the facing.
- Take the interfaced facing piece and place it on top of the correct garment piece, with the right sides together and making sure the edges and any notches match. Pin in place.
- Machine stitch along the relevant edge, taking the recommended seam allowance.
- Snip into the seam allowance and any inward corners, and snip off any outer corners. Snip into any strongly curving seams. Understitch the seam allowance to the facing (see right) at any area on the garment where the facing might roll over the seam edge and so be visible on the right side.
- Turn up the remaining raw edge of the facing by 1cm and to the wrong side. Press the turning so it has a crisp edge.
- Turn under the facing to the wrong side of the garment. If there are any corners, use your little finger or the end of a knitting needle to push the points out. Press.
- You can use topstitching (see p.87) to hold the facing in place. Topstitch along the outer edge of the faced piece, then turn the garment to the wrong side and machine stitch along the turned-under edge of the facing.

Sewing Secrets

To get a neat finish, you could use a professional dressmaking technique known as block fusing. Cut out a bit of fabric that's roughly big enough for your facing piece, then cut a piece of interfacing about the same size. Fuse the fabric and interfacing together. Position the pattern piece on top of the fused layers, pin and cut out.

Understitching

This technique is used on any area where the facing might roll over the seam edge and so be visible on the right side of the garment. Front openings and armholes are typical areas where understitching is used. The understitching secures the facing to the seam allowance and prevents it rolling outwards. The sewing is done on the inside parts of the garment and so is invisible on the right side.

After sewing the seam that joins the facing to the garment piece, press that seam allowance towards the facing. Then machine stitch along the seam allowance about 5mm in from the stitching line – you will be sewing through the seam allowance and the facing. When you turn the facing under to the wrong side of the garment, the stitching will be on the inside.

89

Gather, dart or pleat?

Using gathering will help you when you need to fit a larger piece of fabric into a smaller section.

Bust darts are used to shape the front of a garment and are placed just below the underarm.

Single pleats are formed by one fold of fabric, while box and inverted pleats are formed by two folds in the fabric being brought together.

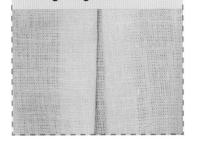

Shaping techniques

Sometimes it is necessary to add some shaping to a garment during construction, either to improve the fit or to add a design detail, and there are various options available.

When you are constructing a garment there are times when you may want to add some shaping by reducing some of the fullness of the fabric at strategic points. There are several ways in which you can do this.

Gathering

With gathering, the extra fullness in a garment piece is reduced by drawing up the fabric – usually along one edge.

• To gather an edge by machine, set the stitch length on your sewing machine to the longest stitch there is. Stitch along the edge 1cm in from the raw edge of the fabric: leave long loose ends of thread at either end of the stitching. Stitch again, just inside the first line of stitching. Wind the loose threads at one end of both lines of stitching around a pin and insert this in the fabric. Pull on the loose threads at the other end of the stitching to draw up the fabric. Adjust the gathers so that the fullness is evenly distributed.

• To gather an edge by hand, using a needle and thread, first secure the end of the thread at the end of the edge to be gathered, 1cm in from the raw edge of the fabric. Work a line of small tacking stitches along the edge and then leave a long loose thread at the end. Repeat to work another line of tacking, just inside the first. Take hold of the loose ends of thread and pull them to draw up the fabric, making sure you distribute the fullness evenly.

Darts

Darts are most frequently used when you need to shape a garment to fit a rounded part of the body: unsurprisingly, bust darts are the most common. Darts take a triangular section out of the fabric – the base of the triangle is at the edge of the fabric with the tip of the triangle pointing towards the fullest part of the bust.

• If a garment piece has a dart in it, you must transfer the markings for the dart from the paper pattern onto the wrong side of your fabric piece.

• Fold the dart along the centre, so that you bring together the marked lines along the edges of the dart; pin.

• Stitch along the marked lines, starting at the widest point of the dart, at the fabric edge. Continue stitching to the point of the dart and let the machine run over the end of the fabric. Don't use the reverse stitch function on your machine to secure the thread as this can bunch up the stitching at the end.

• Press the dart to one side. If you place a tailor's ham or rolled up towel under the dart while pressing, you can more effectively press the curve into the fabric.

Pleats

Another way to take out the fullness in a garment is to use pleats. These are folds in the fabric that can be stitched down at one or both ends to hold them in place.

• To make a single pleat, mark it on the wrong side of the fabric piece in the same way you would a dart (see left). Fold the pleat along the centre, bringing together the marked lines; pin. Stitch along the marked lines, securing the stitching at the beginning and end with the reverse stitch function. Press to one side.

• To make a box or inverted pleat, you need to fold two single pleats and then bring the folded edges together. Tack along the folded edges to secure and then machine stitch across the top of the pleats. Remove the tacking. When the pleat is on the right side, it is a box pleat; on the wrong side, it is an inverted pleat.

Tucks

Tucks, like darts and pleats, are made by folding up the excess fabric and stitching the folds in place; they differ in that they are made in groups. As well as reducing the fullness in the fabric, tucks can have a decorative effect. When you add tucks to a garment they are usually all the same width.

• To make tucks, use a ruler and tailor's chalk and draw the fold lines for the tucks as required for the particular garment. If you are making 1cm wide tucks, then the drawn lines should be 2cm apart. Always draw the centre line first and work outwards from that line.

• Fold the fabric along the central line, wrong sides together and pin in place.

• Fold along the remaining lines in the same way and pin. Machine stitch each tuck in place, 1cm in from the fold.

• Press the tucks to one side. You can press tucks so that the tucks to the left of centre face towards the left, and the tucks to the right of the centre face towards the right. Or you can press them all in one direction.

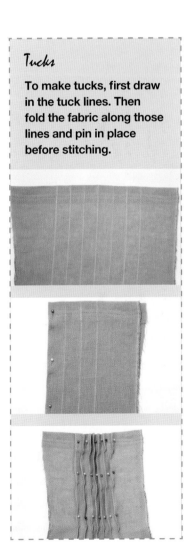

Tucks

To make tucks, first draw in the tuck lines. Then fold the fabric along those lines and pin in place before stitching.

Closures

In dressmaking, there are various ways of holding a garment together at the openings and making sure that it stays put on the right part of your body.

To secure a garment in place when you are wearing it, you need some closures. The clothes in this book use some of the simplest forms of closure there are.

Ties

A narrow length of fabric, tied to another narrow length of fabric, is probably one of the easiest ways to hold garment parts in place. Several of the clothes in this book – such as the side-buttoned jacket (see pp.38–41) or the wrap-over tunic (see pp.22–25) – use ties.

• To make a tie, first cut a length of fabric as given in the pattern.

• Turn under one short end of the fabric strip by 5mm; press.

• Turn under one long edge of the fabric strip by 5mm; press. Turn under and press the other long edge in the same way.

• Fold the strip in half lengthways, wrong sides together, and pin. Topstitch along the short end and down the long turned edges, close to the fold.

Buttons and buttonholes

These traditional types of closure give a neat and tidy finish, and help make a garment look more tailored.

• Start by marking the position of the buttonholes as directed by the sewing pattern. The buttonholes are usually made last, so this is one set of markings that you usually transfer to the fabric pieces after the garment has been constructed. If you marked the buttonholes at the beginning of the construction process, the chalk might wear off.

• To get the right-sized buttonholes, first measure the diameter of your buttons. Then measure the thickness and multiply that by two. Add this figure to the diameter measurement to get the desired length of buttonhole.

• Following the instructions in your sewing machine manual, fit the correct foot to your machine and make the first buttonhole. Then go on to make all the rest, making sure that the ends of the buttonholes line up neatly along the garment.

- Use a seam ripper to slit the fabric inside the buttonholes.
- Bring the part of the garment with the buttonholes to overlap the part where you want the buttons. Pin it in place.
- Push a chalk marker through the first buttonhole, at the centre, to make a mark on the fabric underneath.
- Stitch the first button at the marked position (see right).
- Push the first button through the first buttonhole. Then mark the position of the second buttonhole, as before; stitch the second button in place. Continue in this way until all buttons are stitched.

Elasticated waists

An elasticated waist is one of the simplest ways to hold a skirt or pair of trousers in place. The skirt or trousers are full at the waist and this fullness is gathered in by the elastic. Since the elastic stretches, you can pull the garment wide at the waist to put them on, and once on it will sit comfortably at your natural waistline.

- You will need enough elastic to fit comfortably around your waist when slightly stretched, plus a little extra to overlap at the ends.
- The elastic then needs to be concealed within a channel of fabric; this is known as a casing.
- The simplest way to create a casing is to turn under the fabric and the waistline and stitch this down.
- Turn under the top edge of the garment at the waist by 1cm and press all round.
- Turn under the edge again by the width of the elastic; pin and press.
- Machine stitch all round the turned edge, close to the fold, leaving a gap of about 7.5cm in the stitching.
- Take your elastic and safety pin one end to the waist at the opening. Then put a safety pin in the other end of the elastic and thread the safety pin through the casing – the first safety pin should hold the elastic in place so it doesn't get lost in the casing.
- When the elastic is threaded all the way round the casing, overlap the ends and use one of the safety pins to secure.
- Try on the garment to make sure you are happy with the fit. Once you are, machine or hand sew the overlapping ends of the elastic together.
- Then machine or hand stitch across the opening in the casing.

Sewing on a button

Use this technique for sewing on a holed button. Thread your needle with a double strand of thread and secure the thread on the wrong side of the garment, close to where the button will be. Bring the needle and thread through to the right side at the marked button position. Insert the needle in the first hole on the button from the underside, then insert the needle in the second hole from the top side. Take the needle back down through the fabric. After making this first stitch, slide a cocktail stick or spent match under the button so it passes through the stitch. Continue to stitch through the holes and fabric until the button feels secure; about 10 times should do it. Then remove the cocktail stick and wrap the thread round and round the stitches under the button so that the button is raised above the fabric. This technique ensures the button will not sit too tight inside the buttonhole.

With a shank button, there is no need to do this, since the shank raises the button high enough.

EASY-SEW PATTERNS

In this chapter you will find all the pattern pieces needed for the Bold & Beautiful garments, along with diagrams that show how to lay the pattern pieces out on the fabric, and instructions on how to scale up the patterns to the right size.

How to use this chapter

For a full range of pattern sizes, set up to print easily on A4 paper, use the CD included with this book. If you prefer to scale up a pattern, or enlarge by photocopying, this chapter gives you one size for each project (see chart on p.7), plus diagrams to show how best to lay out the pieces on the fabric.

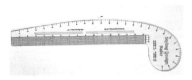

Dot-and-cross paper is marked with evenly spaced dots and crosses. You will need paper where the dots and crosses are spaced 2cm apart to scale up the patterns in this chapter.

When you need to draw in curved lines on your scaled-up pattern, a curved ruler would be very useful. If you don't have one, you will have to plot as many points as possible around the curve and then join the points together by hand.

There are two ways to enlarge pattern pieces to the correct size: scaling them up, or photocopying to a specified percentage.

Scaling up a pattern piece

The pattern pieces in this chapter are on a squared grid. Each square represents 2cm; a heavy line every 10cm makes counting easier. You will therefore need paper which features squares measuring 2cm. You can use squared pattern paper, or dot-and-cross paper. The latter (also known as spot-and-cross paper) is marked with evenly spaced dots and crosses, so you will need paper where the dots and crosses are 2cm apart. If you can't get hold of pattern paper, you can use graph paper with 2cm squares. Squared pattern paper and dot-and-cross paper usually come in large sheets, while graph paper is more likely to be A4.

If you have to stick together pieces of marked pattern paper or graph paper, do this as accurately as possible so that the lines, squares, or dots and crosses on all pieces of paper are evenly lined up. If you fail to do this, it

won't be possible to accurately redraw the pattern pieces on the marked paper.

• Count how many squares wide the piece is on the grid, rounding the number up if partial squares are used. Do the same along the length of the pattern. If your pattern piece is, say, 30 squares wide and 20 squares long make sure you have a piece of squared or dot-and-cross paper that is 10cm more all round than 75cm wide and 50cm long; this ensures you have enough paper with which to work.

• Draw a pencil line along the vertical line on the grid that is closest to the centre of the pattern; do the same with the centre-most horizontal line. (Either the vertical or horizontal line will be parallel to the grain line marked on the pattern piece – which one will depend on the pattern.) Mark the point where these pencil lines bisect with the letter 'A'.

• Find the centre-most vertical line on your squared (or dot-and-cross) paper and draw this in. By counting the squares, calculate the point where the horizontal line on your gridded pattern crosses the vertical line; draw a horizontal line on your paper in the same position. Mark the point where these lines bisect with a letter 'B'.

• On the gridded pattern count the squares between 'A' and the very top of the pattern. On your paper, count the same number of squares (or dots and crosses) up from 'B' and mark this with a pencil cross. If the top of the pattern piece does not fall exactly on a line of the grid, calculate its position between the line above and below; is it halfway between the two, for example, or a third?

• Count the squares between 'A' and the bottom of the pattern. Returning to your paper, count the same number of squares (or dots and crosses) down from 'B' and mark this with a pencil cross. Count the number of squares between 'A' and a point on the side of the pattern – the underarm, for example. On the paper, make a cross the same number of squares from 'B'.

• Continue plotting points around the edge of the pattern on your paper in the same way. The more points you plot, the more accurate your finished scaled-up pattern will be. When you can see clearly the outline of the pattern piece on your paper, join the crosses together. Use a ruler for straight lines and, if you have one, a curved ruler for the curved edges.

• Once you have drawn the outline of the pattern, make sure you transfer the notches, grain line, and any other marks, to the pattern. Count up squares to get the position of the notches and other marks correct; the grain line will be parallel to either the vertical or horizontal lines you drew on the squared (or dot-and-cross) paper at the beginning.

• When you've finished marking up the pattern, cut out the paper piece.

Photocopying a pattern piece

Alternatively, you can photocopy the pattern pieces and enlarge them to the size you want. The percentage enlargement needed to get the correct size is noted below the pattern pieces. Once enlarged, cut out the pattern pieces. This method will involve sticking together quite a number of sheets of paper.

Using the pattern pieces

• Lay out the fabric and position the pattern pieces as indicated by the layout diagram (located on the same page as the gridded pattern pieces). All the patterns in this book are laid out on 140cm width fabric.

• There willl be instances where you have one paper pattern piece but need it to cut out two fabric pieces; for example, when you are cutting out the sleeves. Either make two paper pattern pieces, or use the paper pattern to cut out one fabric piece, then re-pin the paper pattern on the fabric to cut out the second piece.

• When you have the paper patterns in position on the fabric, pin them in place, making sure you line up the marked grain line with the lengthways grain on the fabric (see p.83).

• Cut out the fabric pieces, transferring any notches and other marks to the fabric using tailor's chalk (see p.81).

Pattern marks

The small triangles along the edges of a pattern are the notches. The notches on one pattern piece are matched to the notches on the pattern piece for an adjoining part of the garment. It's important, therefore, to mark notches accurately so that the parts of the garment fit together.

Some of the Bold & Beautiful clothes feature pleats and tucks. Their position on the garment pieces is indicated on the patterns by lines.

In the patterns provided you will also find templates to help you position things like buttonholes and tucks.

The most important mark on a pattern is the grain line. This is a long line with an arrowhead at either end. When you cut out the pattern piece from the fabric, this marked line must be parallel with the fabric grain. (See p.83 for instructions on how to position the pattern on the grain, and on how to mark up the fabric pieces.)

Simple tunic

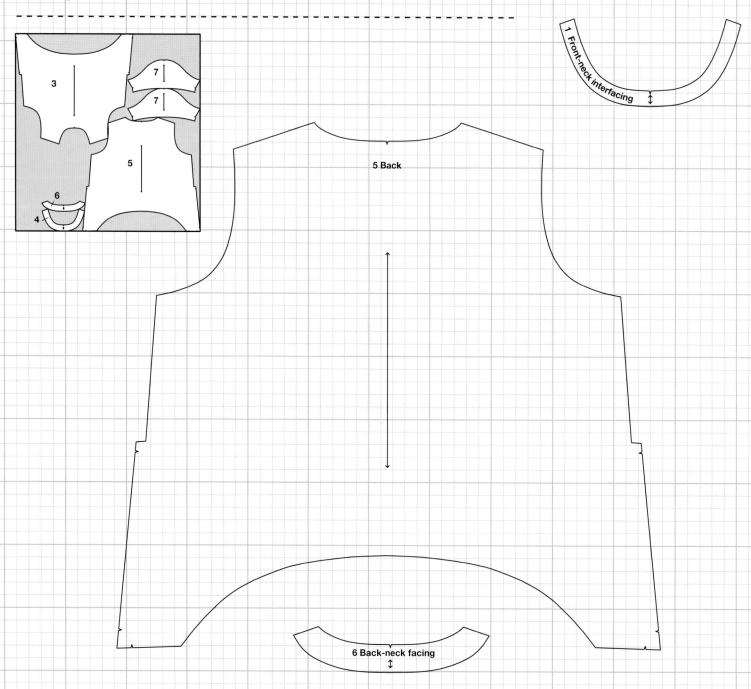

3

7

7

5

6

4

1 Front-neck interfacing

5 Back

6 Back-neck facing

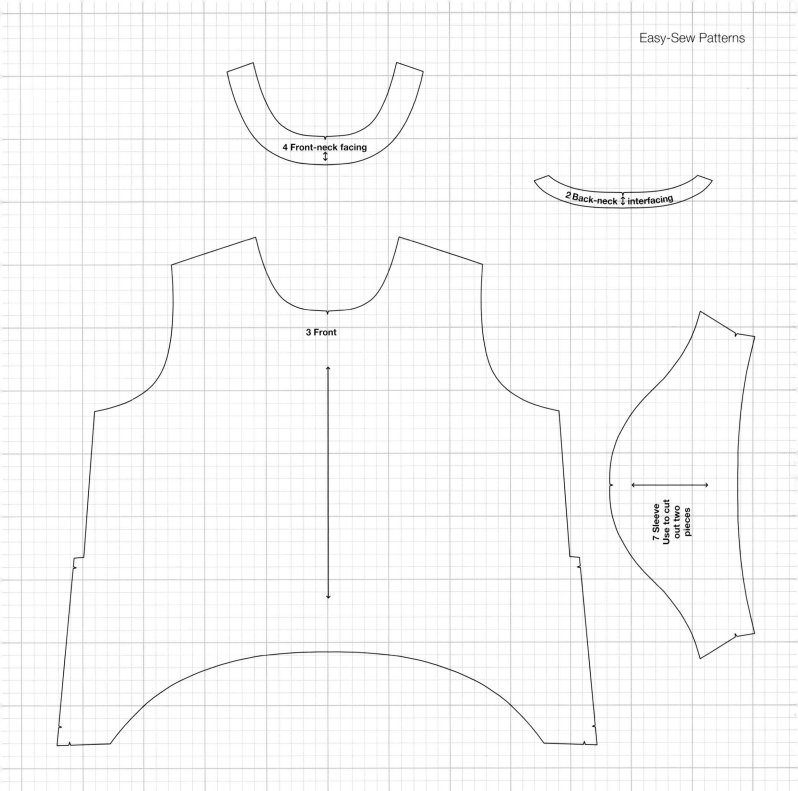

4 Front-neck facing

2 Back-neck interfacing

3 Front

7 Sleeve
Use to cut
out two
pieces

Note: The pieces for this project need to be photocopied at 600 % to be the correct size.

Hankie-hem tunic

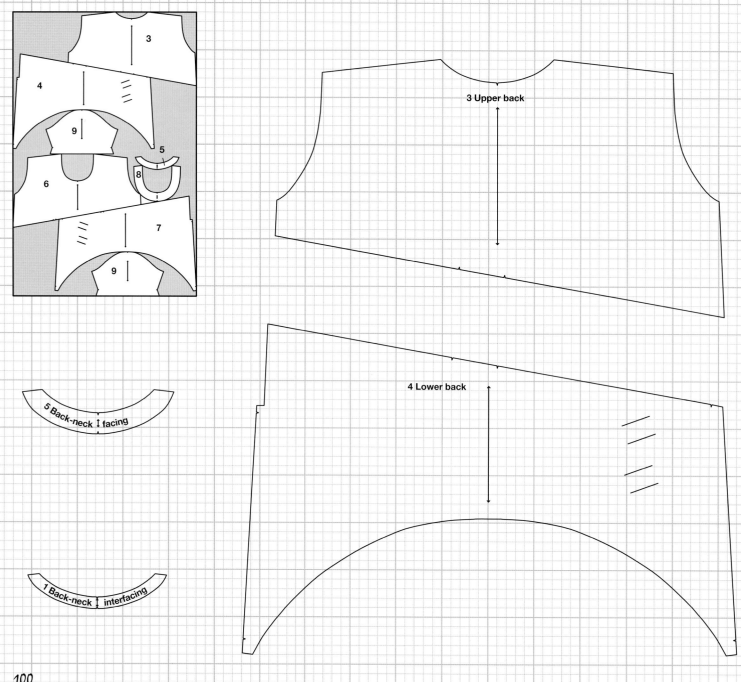

3 Upper back

4 Lower back

5 Back-neck facing

1 Back-neck interfacing

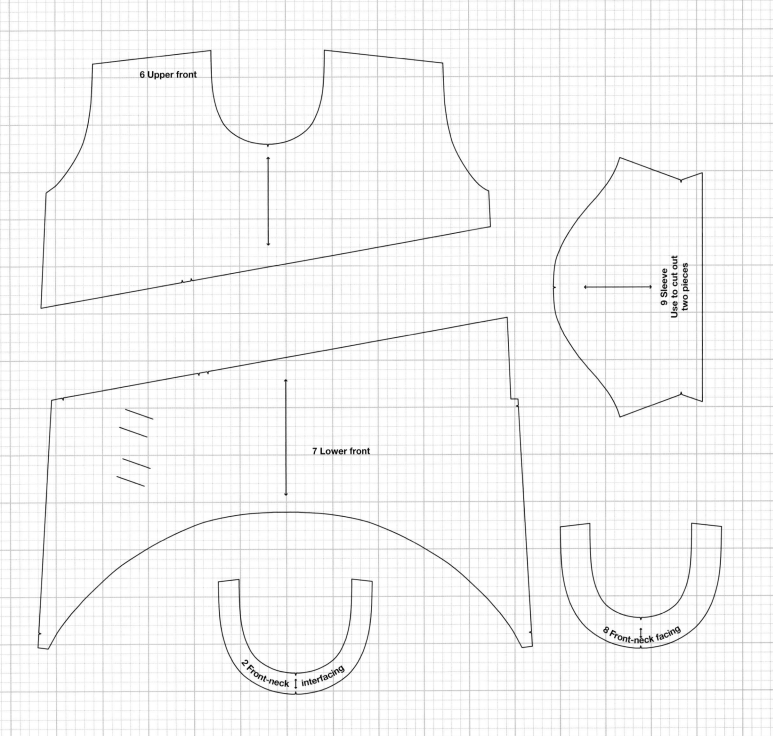

6 Upper front

9 Sleeve
Use to cut out
two pieces

7 Lower front

2 Front-neck interfacing

8 Front-neck facing

Note: The pieces for this project need to be photocopied at 800 % to be the correct size.

Asymmetric tunic

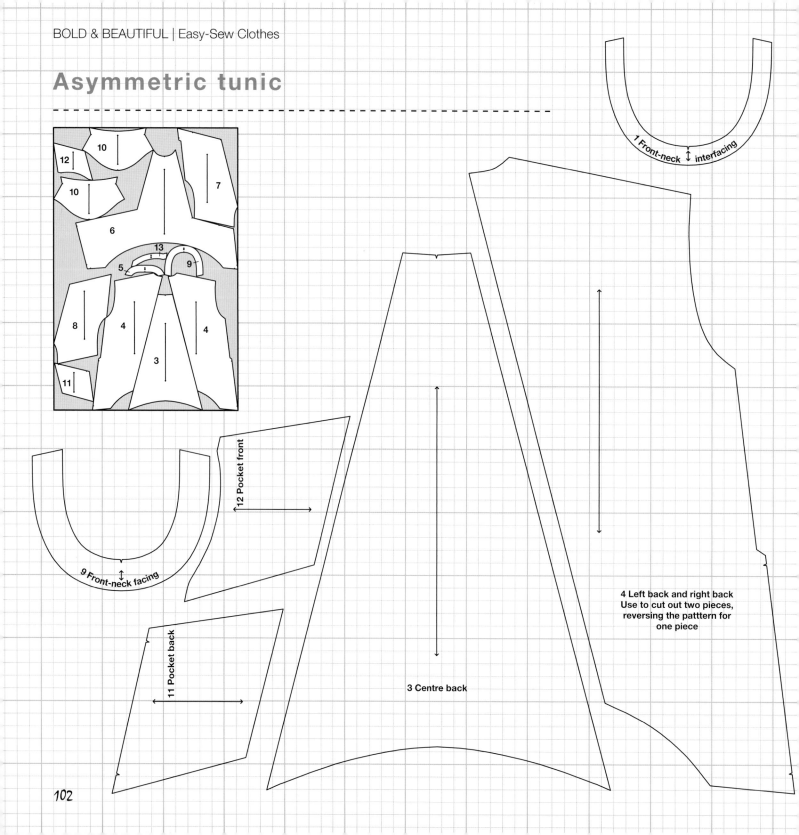

1 Front-neck ↕ interfacing

10

12

10

7

6

13

5

9

8

4

4

3

11

12 Pocket front

9 Front-neck facing

11 Pocket back

3 Centre back

4 Left back and right back
Use to cut out two pieces,
reversing the patttern for
one piece

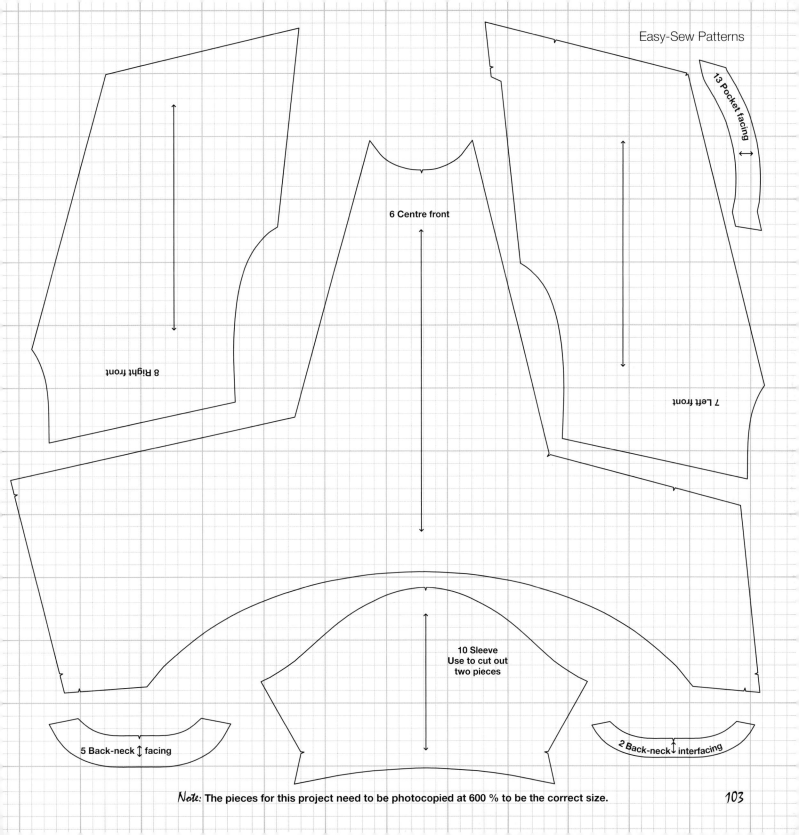

Easy-Sew Patterns

13 Pocket facing

6 Centre front

8 Right front

7 Left front

10 Sleeve
Use to cut out
two pieces

5 Back-neck ↕ facing

2 Back-neck ↕ interfacing

Note: **The pieces for this project need to be photocopied at 600 % to be the correct size.**

Wrap-over tunic

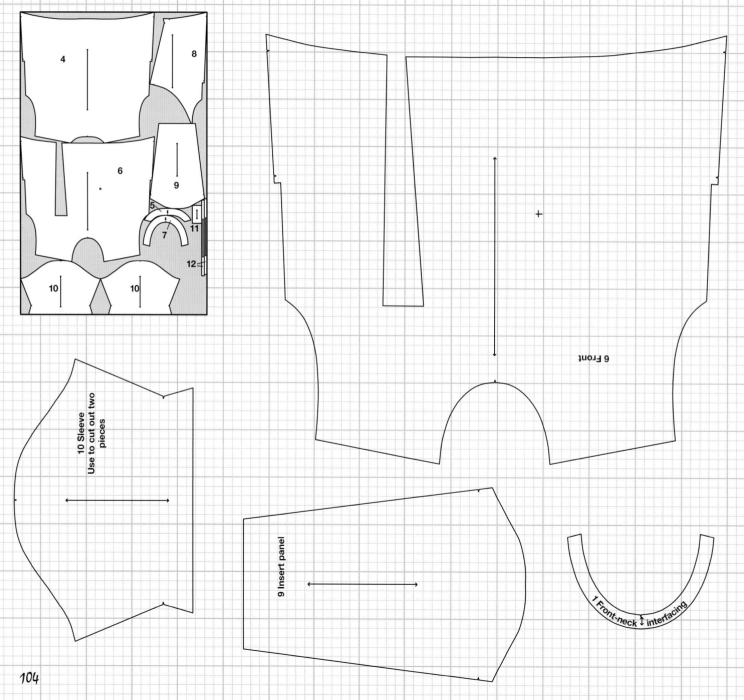

6 Front

10 Sleeve
Use to cut out two pieces

9 Insert panel

1 Front-neck interfacing

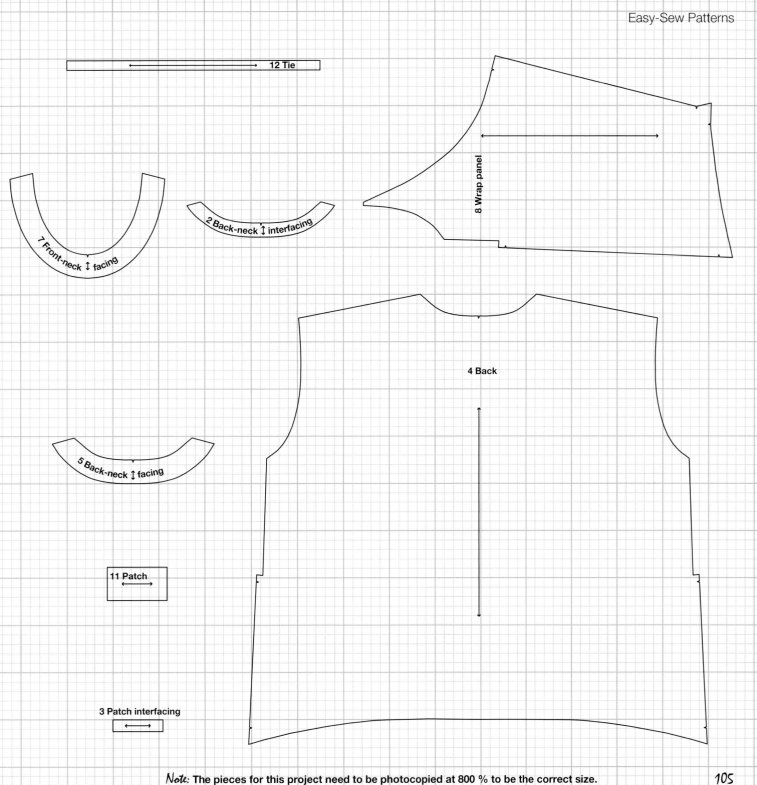

12 Tie

7 Front-neck ↕ facing

2 Back-neck ↕ interfacing

8 Wrap panel

5 Back-neck ↕ facing

4 Back

11 Patch

3 Patch interfacing

Note: **The pieces for this project need to be photocopied at 800 % to be the correct size.**

Tucked dress or tunic

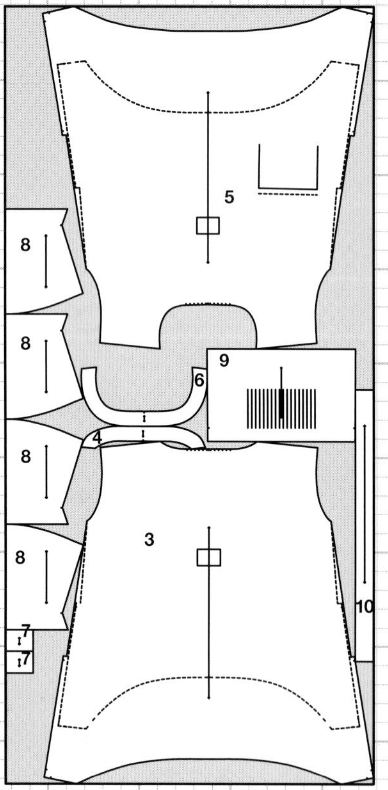

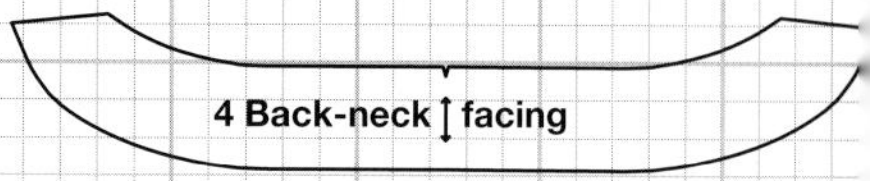

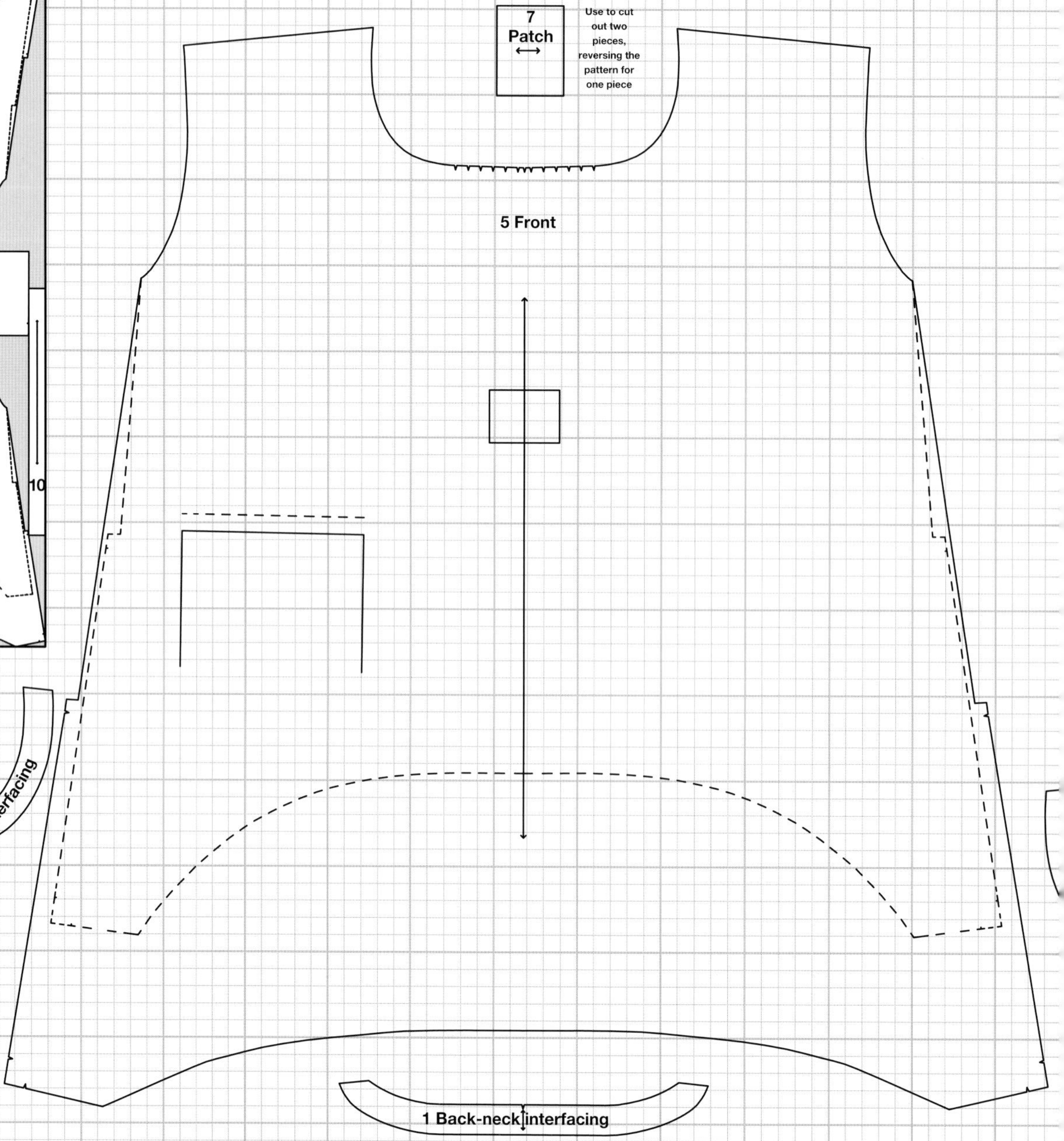

4 Back-neck facing

7
Patch
↔

Use to cut
out two
pieces,
reversing the
pattern for
one piece

5 Front

5

8

8

8

8

9

6

4

3

10

7

7

2 Front-neck interfacing

1 Back-neck interfacing

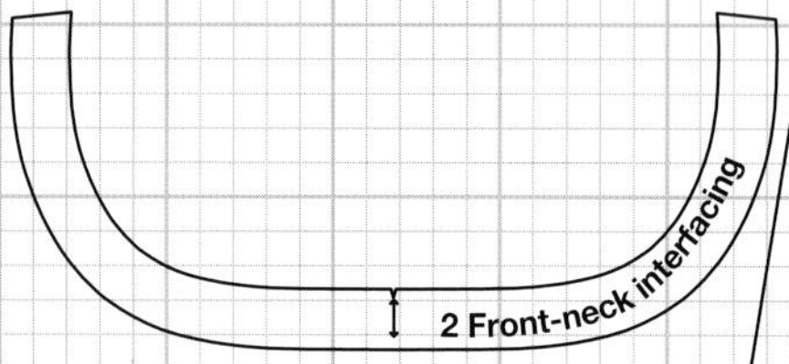

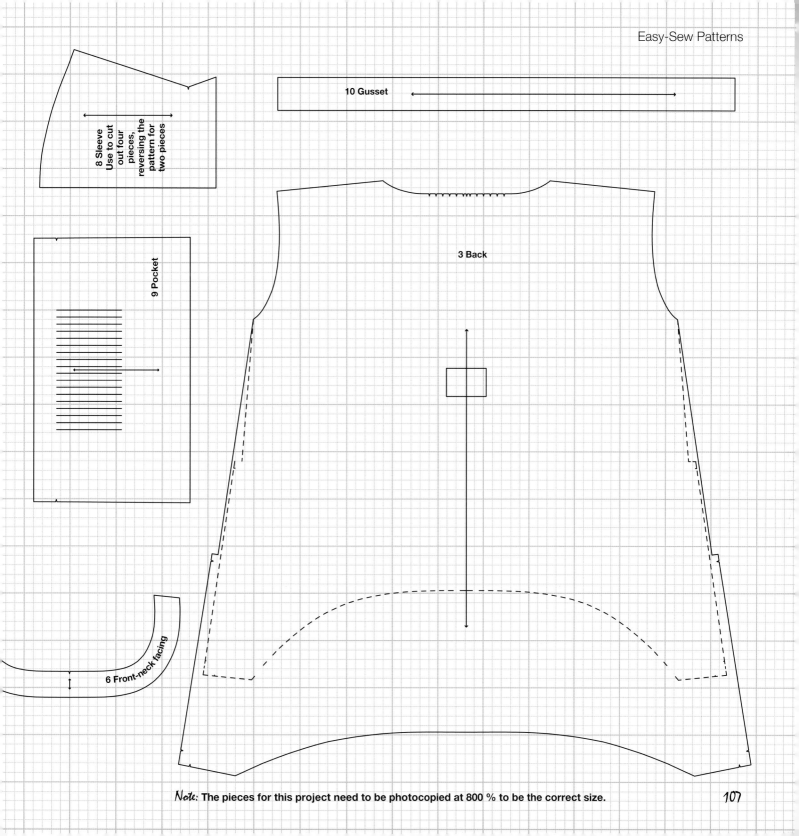

10 Gusset

8 Sleeve
Use to cut out four pieces, reversing the pattern for two pieces

9 Pocket

3 Back

6 Front-neck facing

Note: The pieces for this project need to be photocopied at 800 % to be the correct size.

Asymmetric dress

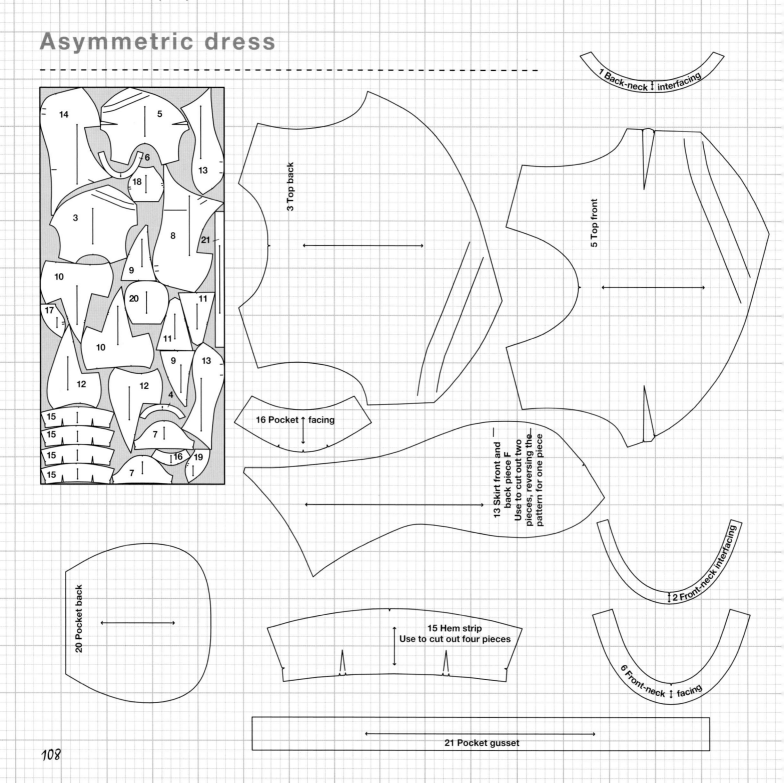

1 Back-neck interfacing

14

5

6

13

18

3

8

21

10

9

11

17

20

11

10

9

13

12

12

4

15

15

7

15

16

19

15

7

3 Top back

5 Top front

16 Pocket facing

13 Skirt front and back piece F
Use to cut out two pieces, reversing the pattern for one piece

2 Front-neck interfacing

6 Front-neck facing

20 Pocket back

15 Hem strip
Use to cut out four pieces

21 Pocket gusset

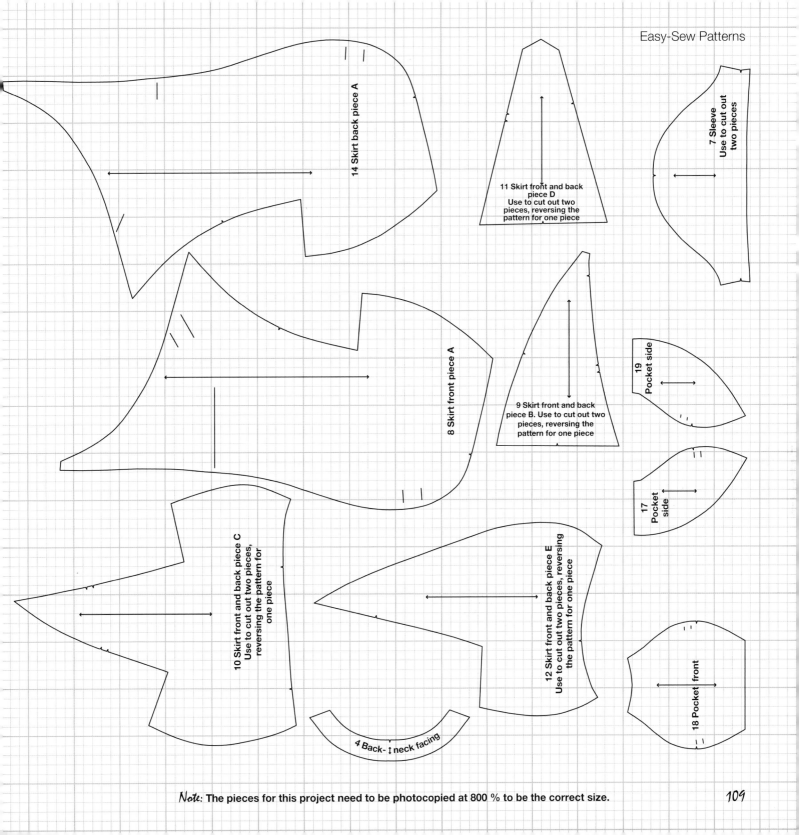

14 Skirt back piece A

11 Skirt front and back piece D
Use to cut out two pieces, reversing the pattern for one piece

7 Sleeve
Use to cut out two pieces

8 Skirt front piece A

9 Skirt front and back piece B. Use to cut out two pieces, reversing the pattern for one piece

19 Pocket side

17 Pocket side

10 Skirt front and back piece C
Use to cut out two pieces, reversing the pattern for one piece

12 Skirt front and back piece E
Use to cut out two pieces, reversing the pattern for one piece

18 Pocket front

4 Back- neck facing

Note: **The pieces for this project need to be photocopied at 800 % to be the correct size.**

Pinafore dress

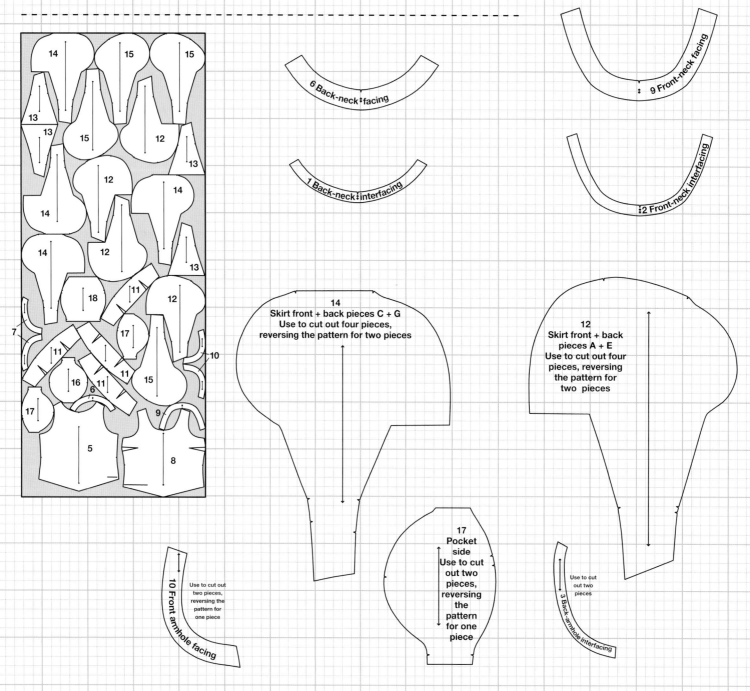

6 Back-neck facing

9 Front-neck facing

1 Back-neck interfacing

2 Front-neck interfacing

14
Skirt front + back pieces C + G
Use to cut out four pieces,
reversing the pattern for two pieces

12
Skirt front + back
pieces A + E
Use to cut out four
pieces, reversing
the pattern for
two pieces

17
Pocket
side
Use to cut
out two
pieces,
reversing
the
pattern
for one
piece

10 Front armhole facing

Use to cut out
two pieces,
reversing the
pattern for
one piece

3 Back-armhole interfacing

Use to cut
out two
pieces

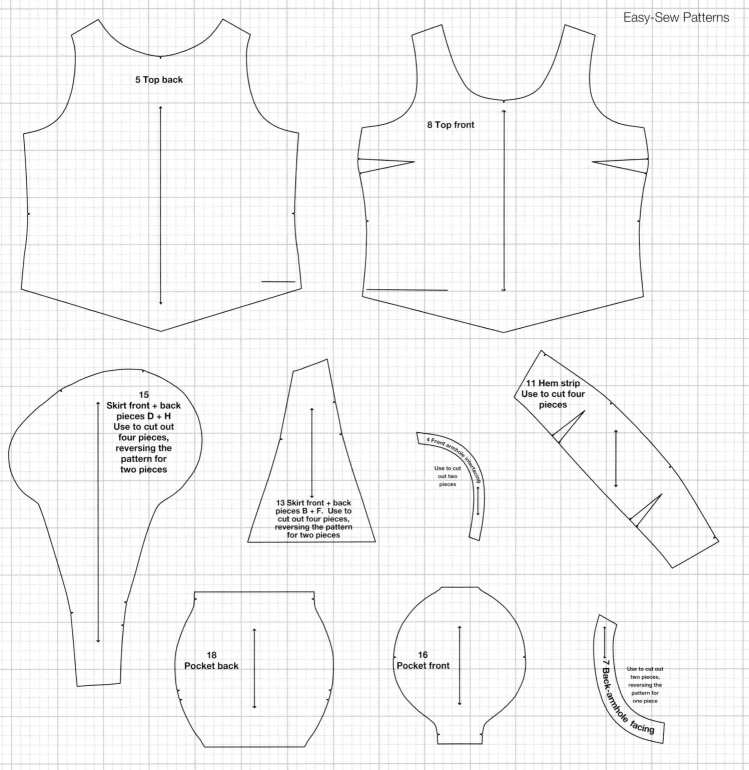

5 Top back

8 Top front

15
Skirt front + back
pieces D + H
Use to cut out
four pieces,
reversing the
pattern for
two pieces

13 Skirt front + back
pieces B + F. Use to
cut out four pieces,
reversing the pattern
for two pieces

4 Front armhole interfacing

Use to cut
out two
pieces

11 Hem strip
Use to cut four
pieces

18
Pocket back

16
Pocket front

7 Back-armhole facing

Use to cut out
two pieces,
reversing the
pattern for
one piece

Note: The pieces for this project need to be photocopied at 800 % to be the correct size.

Side-buttoned jacket

15 Tie
Use to cut out two pieces

16 Box-pleated pocket

5 Right & left back
Use to cut out two pieces, reversing the pattern for one piece

1 Right front-neck interfacing

8 Right front

11 Left front

9 Right front-neck facing

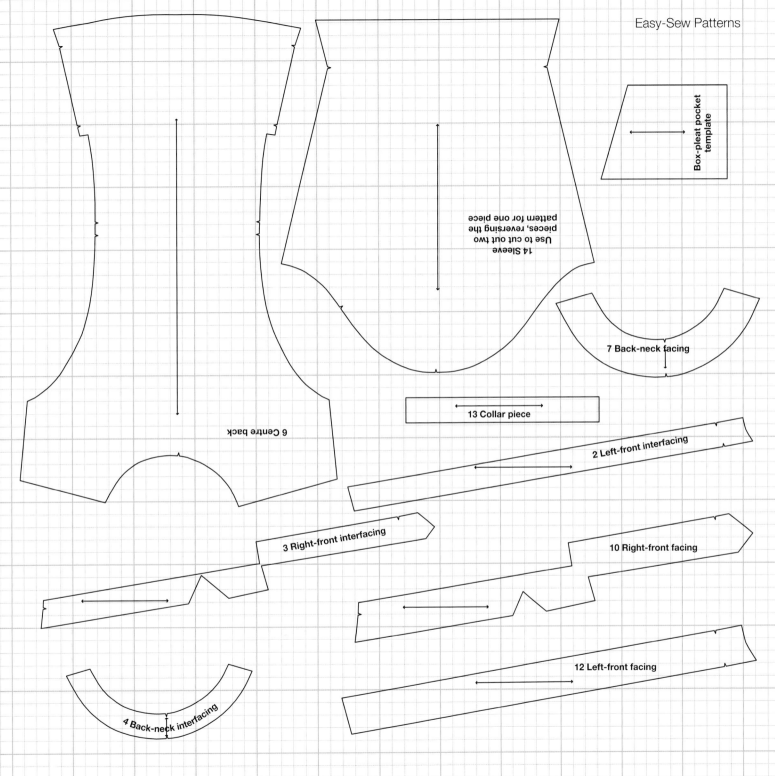

Box-pleat pocket template

14 Sleeve
Use to cut out two pieces, reversing the pattern for one piece

7 Back-neck facing

13 Collar piece

6 Centre back

2 Left-front interfacing

3 Right-front interfacing

10 Right-front facing

12 Left-front facing

4 Back-neck interfacing

Note: The pieces for this project need to be photocopied at 600 % to be the correct size.

Waistcoat

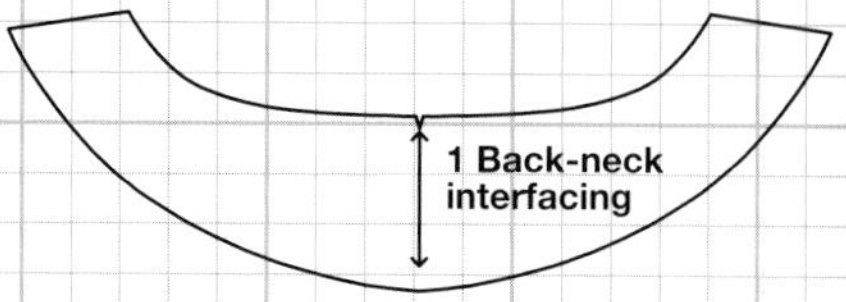

1 Back-neck
interfacing

20
18
14
16
15
13
12
8
5
6
4
16
16
11
10
9
11
7
7
19

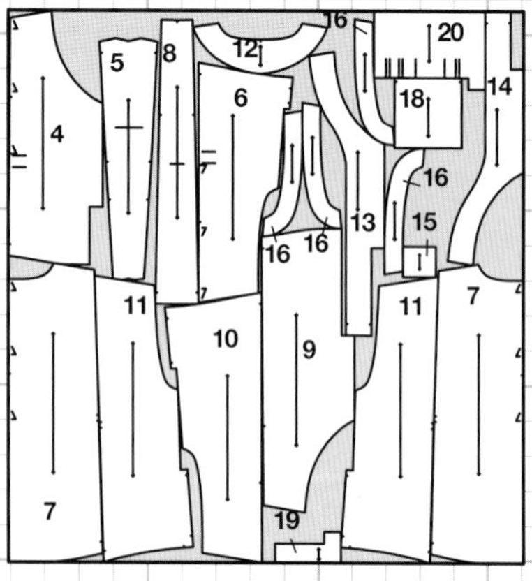

12 Back-neck
facing

10 Left-front piece G

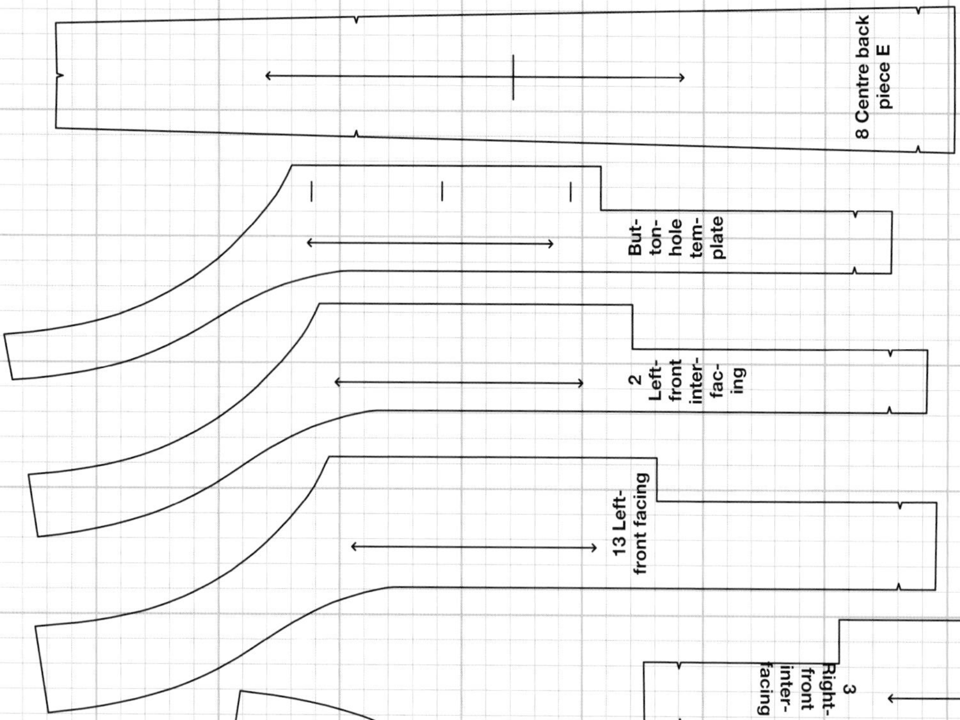

8 Centre back
piece E
But-
ton-
hole
tem-
plate
2
Left-
front
inter-
fac-
ing
13 Left-
front facing

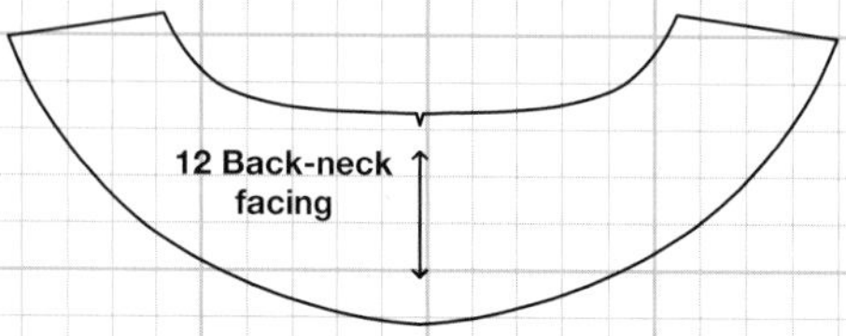

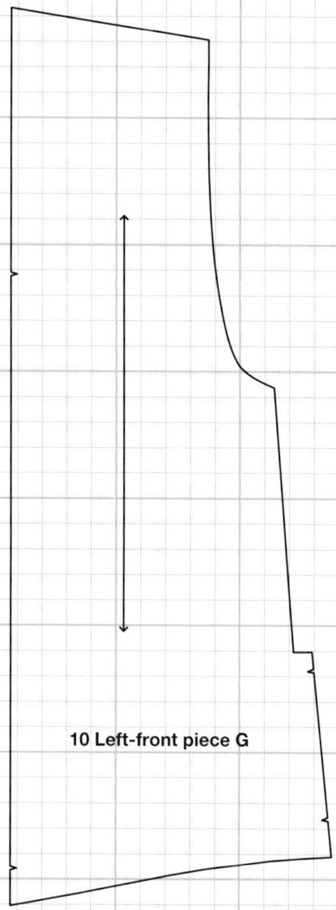

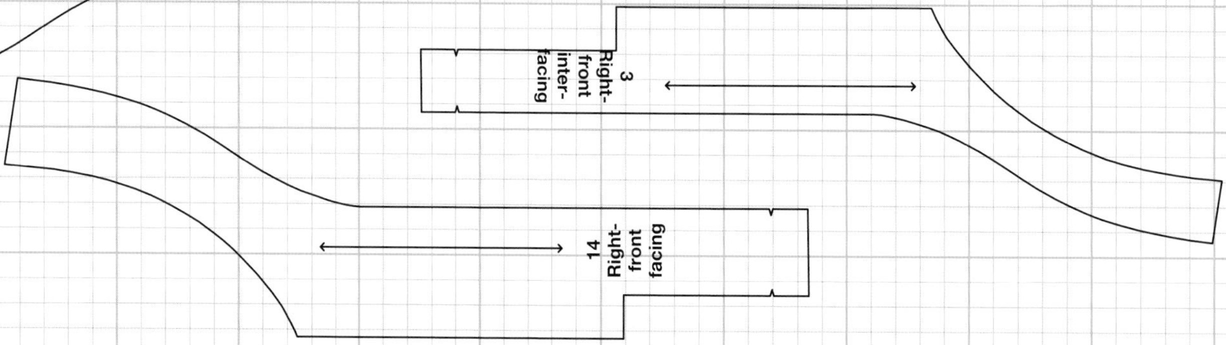

3
Right-
front
inter-
facing
14
Right-
front
facing

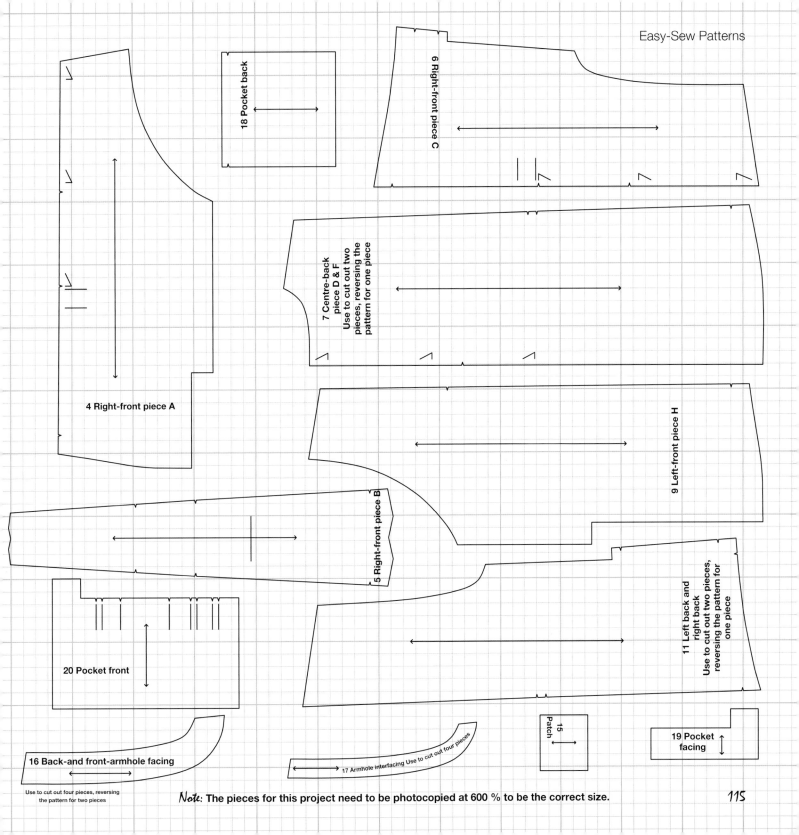

Easy-Sew Patterns

18 Pocket back

6 Right-front piece C

7 Centre-back piece D & F
Use to cut out two pieces, reversing the pattern for one piece

4 Right-front piece A

9 Left-front piece H

5 Right-front piece B

11 Left back and right back
Use to cut out two pieces, reversing the pattern for one piece

20 Pocket front

16 Back-and front-armhole facing

17 Armhole interfacing Use to cut out four pieces

15 Patch

19 Pocket facing

Use to cut out four pieces, reversing the pattern for two pieces

Note: The pieces for this project need to be photocopied at 600 % to be the correct size.

115

Kimono jacket

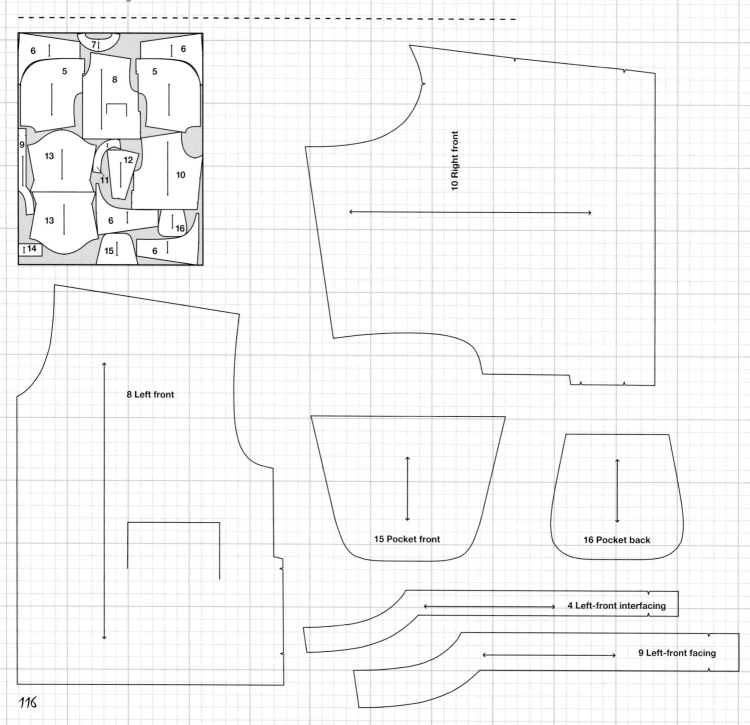

10 Right front

8 Left front

15 Pocket front

16 Pocket back

4 Left-front interfacing

9 Left-front facing

6 5 7 6 5 8 9 13 11 12 10 13 6 16 14 15 6

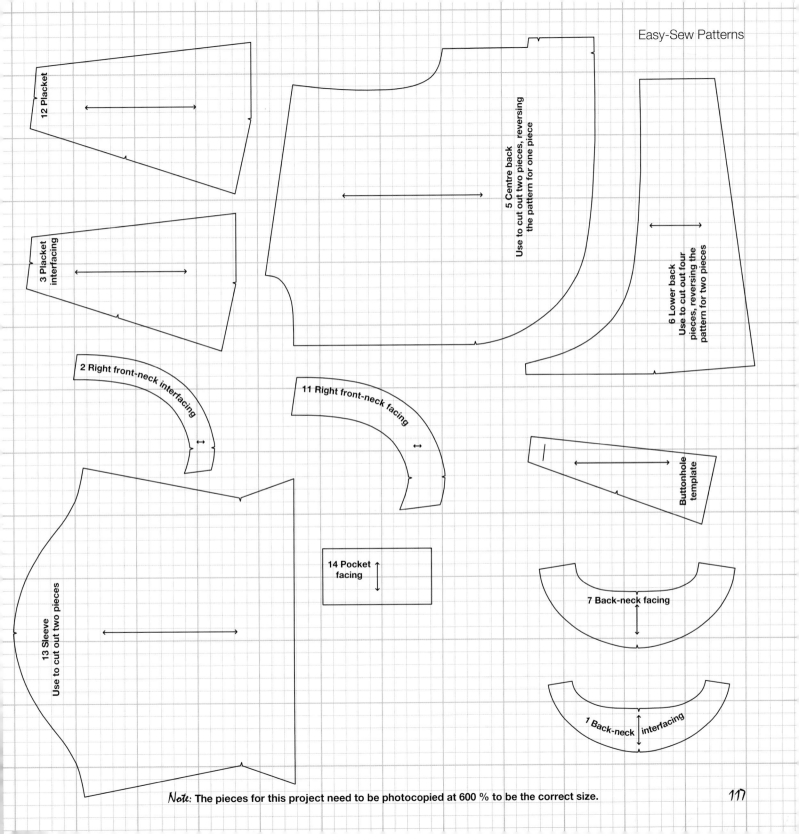

12 Placket

3 Placket interfacing

5 Centre back
Use to cut out two pieces, reversing the pattern for one piece

6 Lower back
Use to cut out four pieces, reversing the pattern for two pieces

2 Right front-neck interfacing

11 Right front-neck facing

Buttonhole template

14 Pocket facing

7 Back-neck facing

13 Sleeve
Use to cut out two pieces

1 Back-neck interfacing

Note: The pieces for this project need to be photocopied at 600 % to be the correct size.

117

Yoked jacket

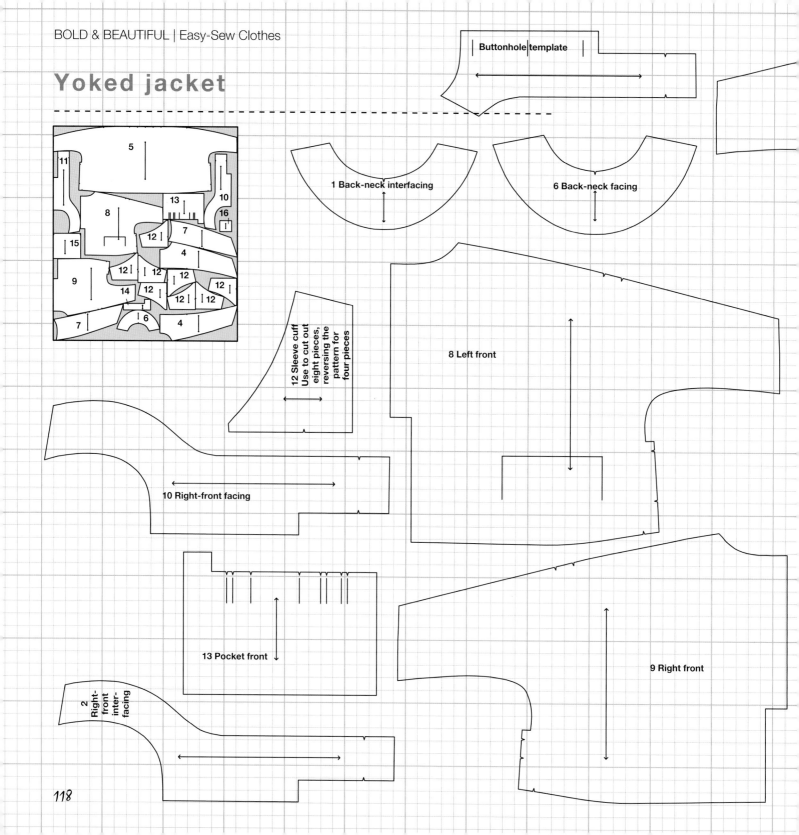

Buttonhole template

1 Back-neck interfacing

6 Back-neck facing

12 Sleeve cuff
Use to cut out
eight pieces,
reversing the
pattern for
four pieces

8 Left front

10 Right-front facing

13 Pocket front

2 Right-front inter-facing

9 Right front

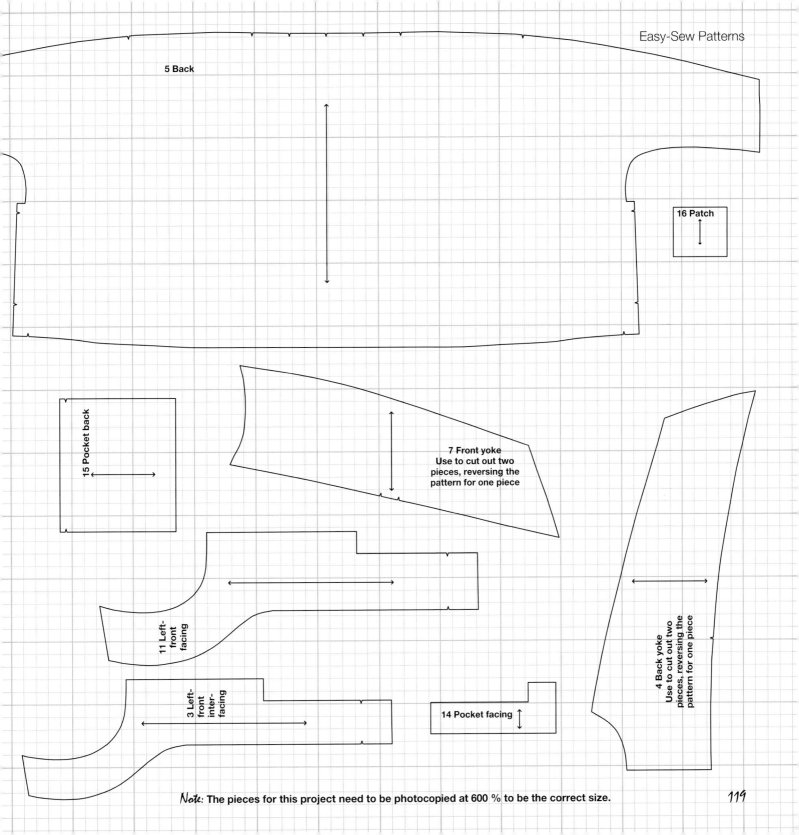

5 Back

16 Patch

15 Pocket back

7 Front yoke
Use to cut out two
pieces, reversing the
pattern for one piece

11 Left-
front
facing

3 Left-
front
inter-
facing

14 Pocket facing

4 Back yoke
Use to cut out two
pieces, reversing the
pattern for one piece

Note: The pieces for this project need to be photocopied at 600 % to be the correct size.

119

Buttoned coat

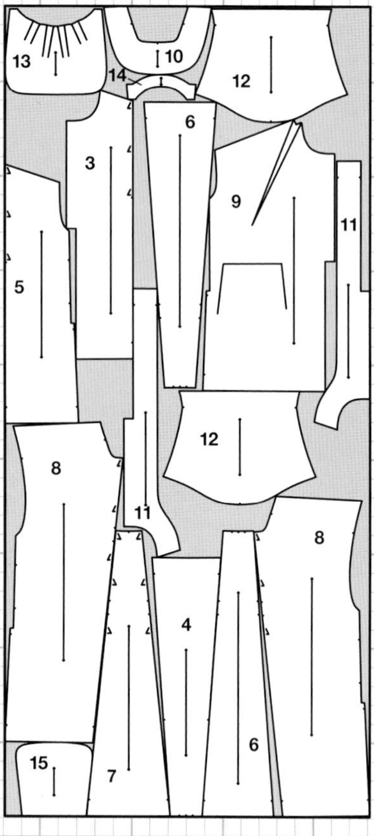

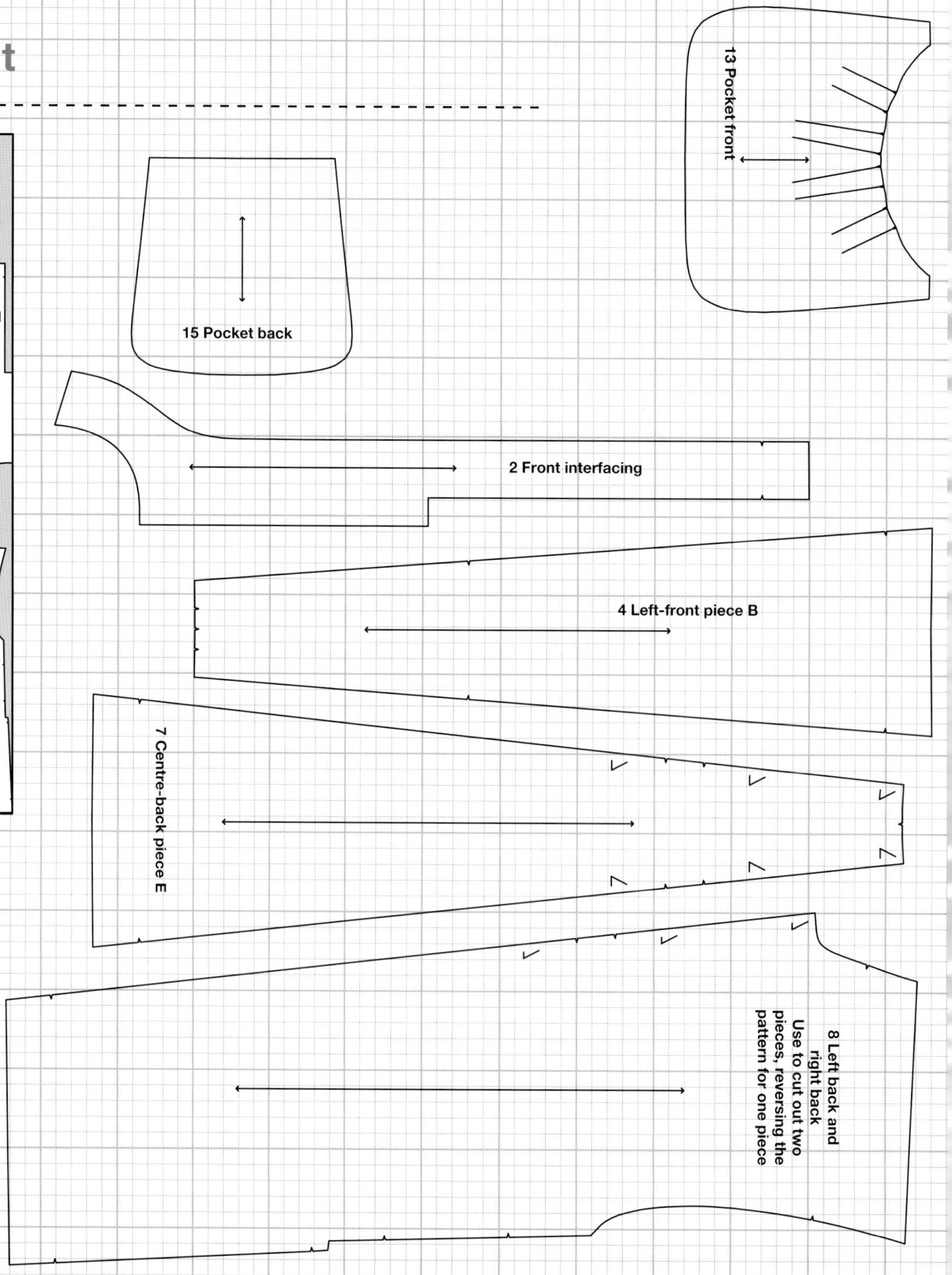

13 Pocket front

13

14

10

12

6

3

9

11

5

12

8

11

8

15

7

4

6

15 Pocket back

2 Front interfacing

4 Left-front piece B

7 Centre-back piece E

10 Back-neck facing

8 Left back and right back
Use to cut out two pieces, reversing the pattern for one piece

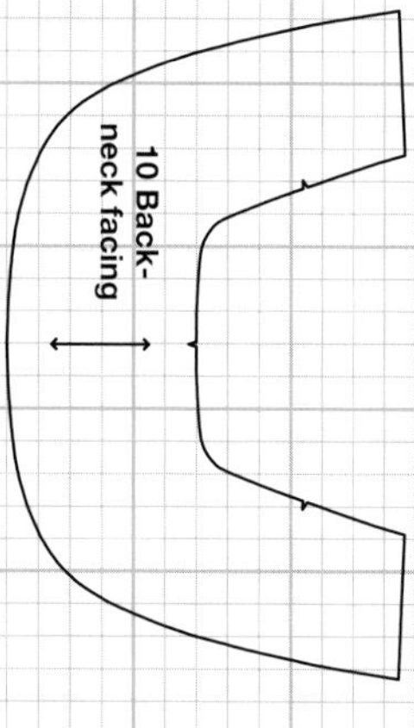

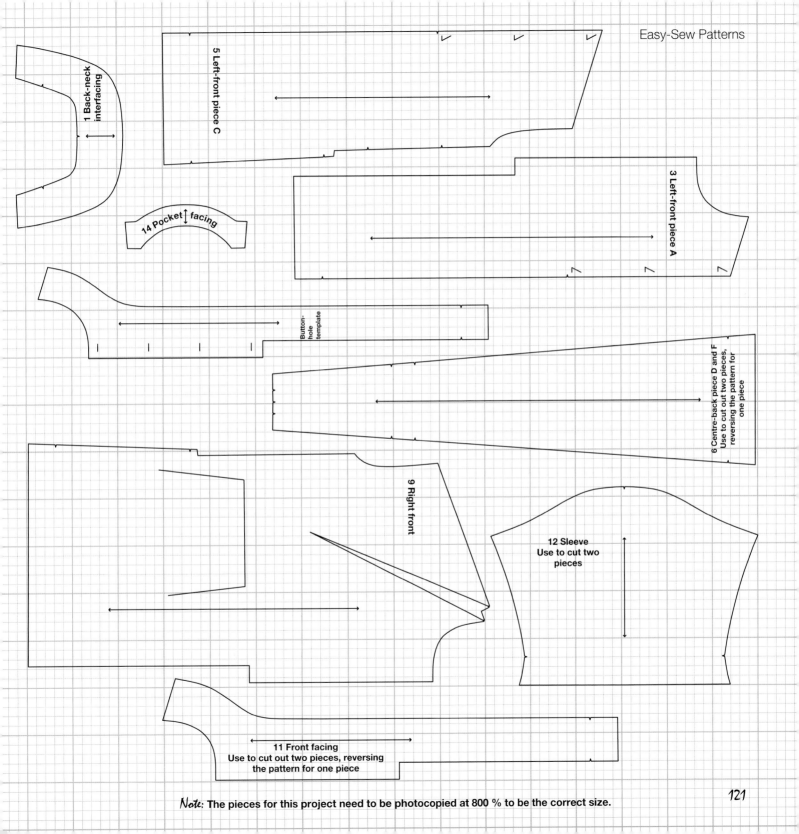

Easy-Sew Patterns

1 Back-neck interfacing

5 Left-front piece C

3 Left-front piece A

14 Pocket facing

Button-hole template

6 Centre-back piece D and F
Use to cut out two pieces,
reversing the pattern for
one piece

9 Right front

12 Sleeve
Use to cut two
pieces

11 Front facing
Use to cut out two pieces, reversing
the pattern for one piece

Note: The pieces for this project need to be photocopied at 800 % to be the correct size.

121

Gathered skirt

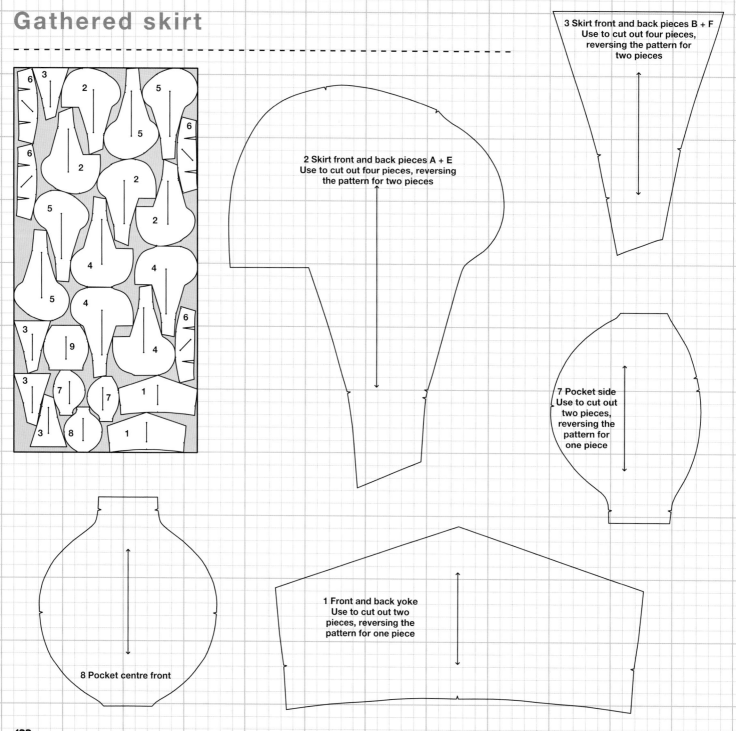

3 Skirt front and back pieces B + F
Use to cut out four pieces, reversing the pattern for two pieces

2 Skirt front and back pieces A + E
Use to cut out four pieces, reversing the pattern for two pieces

7 Pocket side
Use to cut out two pieces, reversing the pattern for one piece

8 Pocket centre front

1 Front and back yoke
Use to cut out two pieces, reversing the pattern for one piece

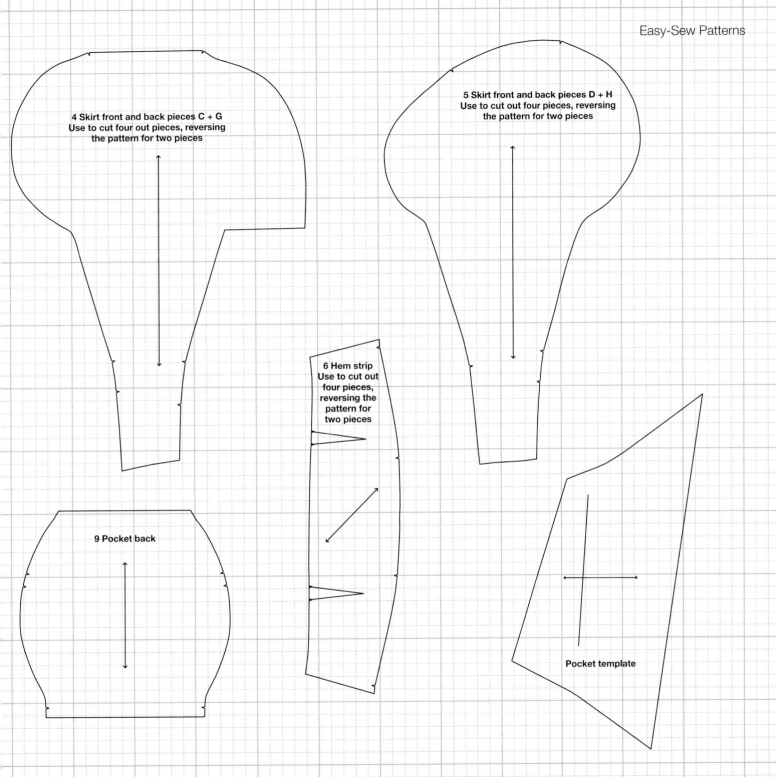

4 Skirt front and back pieces C + G
Use to cut four out pieces, reversing
the pattern for two pieces

5 Skirt front and back pieces D + H
Use to cut out four pieces, reversing
the pattern for two pieces

6 Hem strip
Use to cut out
four pieces,
reversing the
pattern for
two pieces

9 Pocket back

Pocket template

Note: **The pieces for this project need to be photocopied at 600 % to be the correct size.**

Harem pants

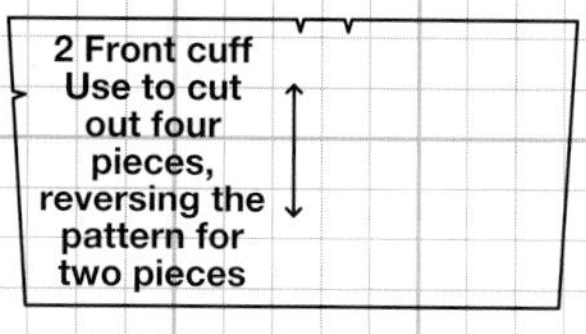

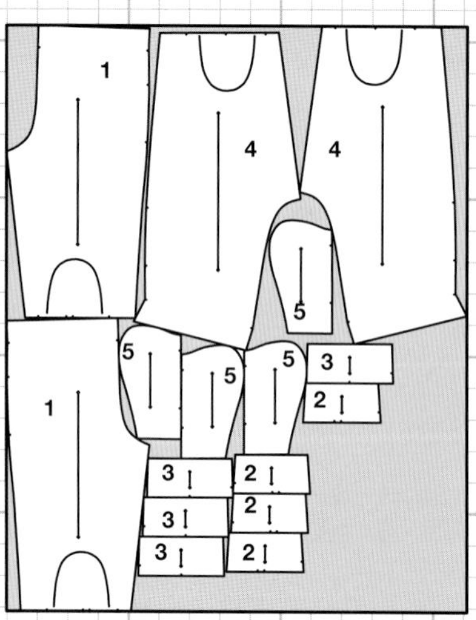

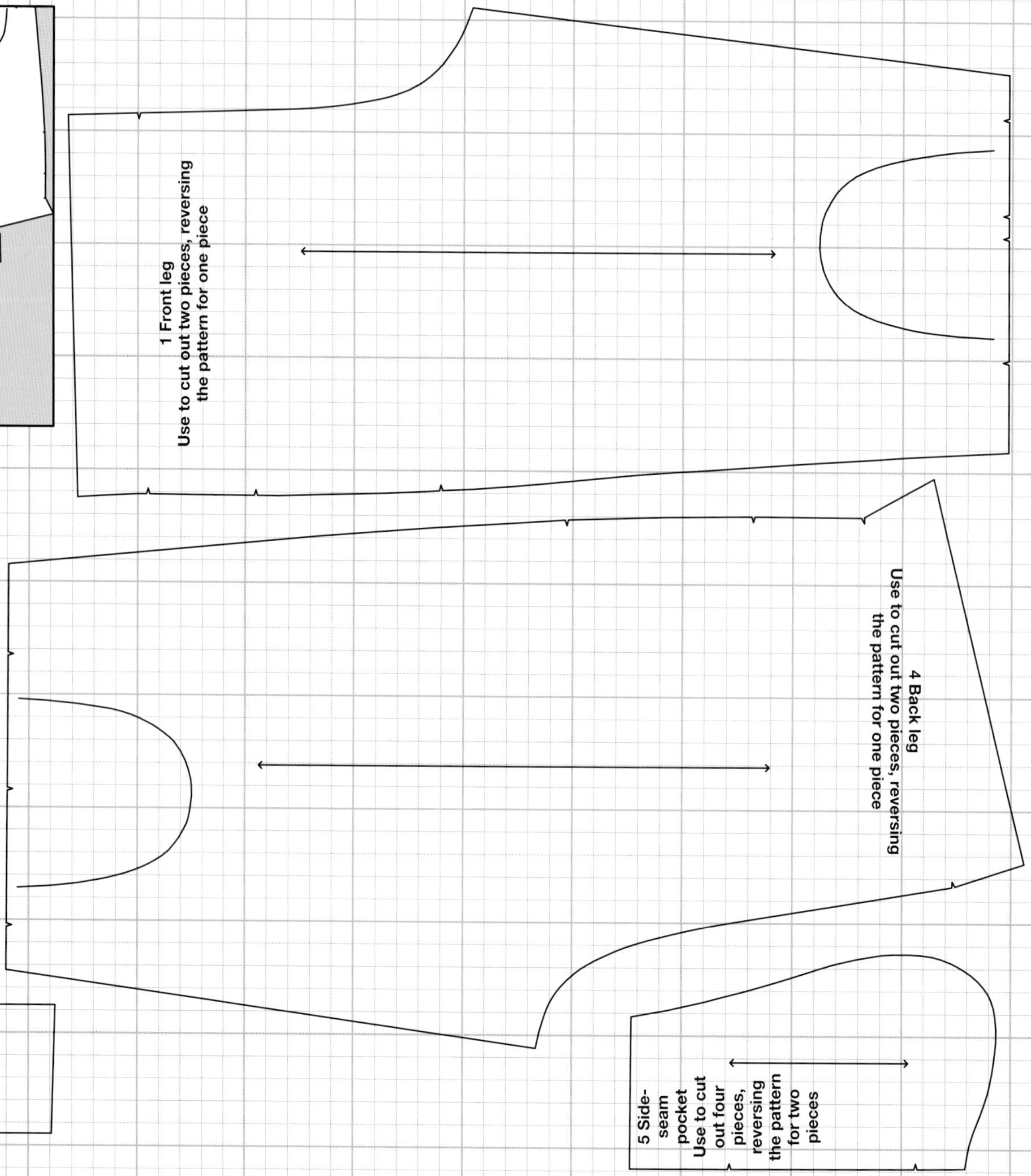

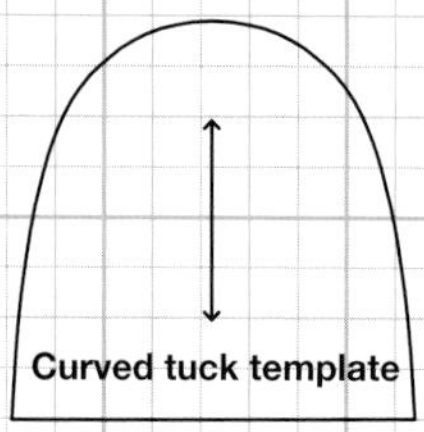

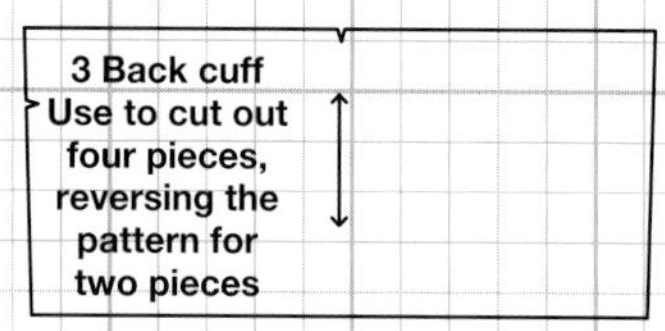

2 Front cuff
Use to cut
out four
pieces,
reversing the
pattern for
two pieces

1

4

4

5

5

5

5

3

2

1

1

3

2

3

3

2

2

3

2

1 Front leg
Use to cut out two pieces, reversing
the pattern for one piece

4 Back leg
Use to cut out two pieces, reversing
the pattern for one piece

Curved tuck template

3 Back cuff
Use to cut out
four pieces,
reversing the
pattern for
two pieces

5 Side-
seam
pocket
Use to cut
out four
pieces,
reversing
the pattern
for two
pieces

124   *Note*: The pieces for this project need to be photocopied at 600 % to be the correct size.

Wide-leg trousers

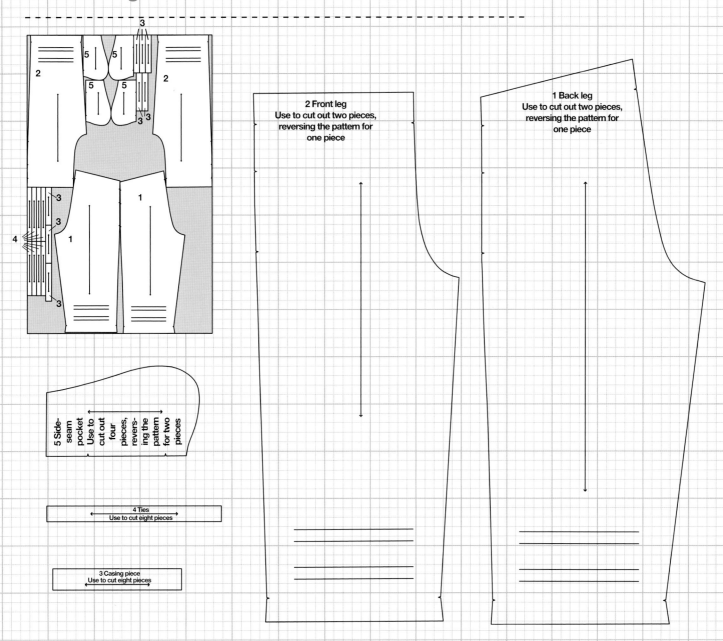

2 Front leg
Use to cut out two pieces,
reversing the pattern for
one piece

1 Back leg
Use to cut out two pieces,
reversing the pattern for
one piece

5 Side-seam pocket Use to cut out four pieces, reversing the pattern for two pieces

4 Ties
Use to cut eight pieces

3 Casing piece
Use to cut eight pieces

Note: **The pieces for this project need to be photocopied at 800 % to be the correct size.**

Index

ACKNOWLEDGMENTS

I wish to thank all those who have helped me to make this book possible. Caroline Smith was fantastic in helping me write the book and style the photography. She has been very helpful and thoroughly enjoyable to work with. Thank you to Dogan Arabaci and Gulcan Comak of Bil-Kon Computer Company in Turkey. They spent a great deal of time making sure the pattern details were exactly right. Their expertise was invaluable and I very much appreciate their dedication.

My thanks to Violeta for helping put together the clothing samples.

To Helen for her constant support and always being ready to help out.

Thanks to the team at Quantum: Sarah Bloxham for her vision and guidance, Samantha Warrington for ensuring everything happened as it should and Jo Morley for supporting every stage of the process. Also, to Miranda Harrison for being the link in the co-ordination and layout of the book. To Blanche Williams for the beautiful book design, and Stephen Dew for his skilful work creating the pattern layouts. To Rohana Yosuf for ensuring the book was printed to the highest possible standard.

Thank you to my photographer Paul Michael Hughes and to the model Laura Cooper. Also, to Quantum's talented photographer Simon Pask.

And finally, I thank my husband Qamar for his patience and support while I prepared for the publishing of this book.

Habibe Acikgoz

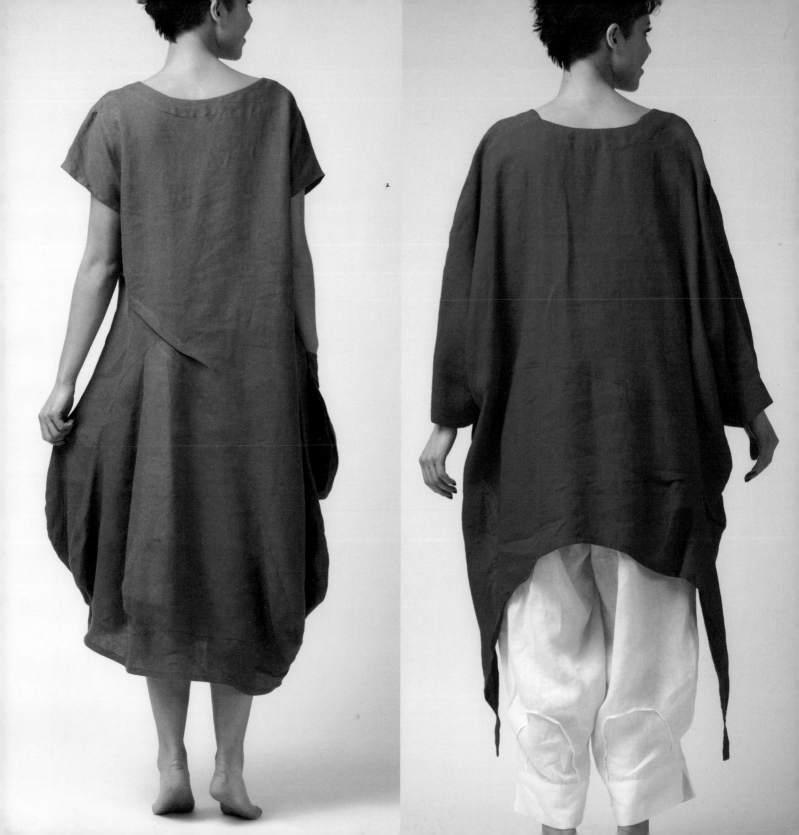